BARTMAN™

THE BEST OF THE BEST!

HarperPerennial
A Division of HarperCollins*Publishers*

To the loving memory of Snowball I:
your secret identity is safe with us.

HarperCollins books may be purchased for educational, business, or sales promotional use. For information, please write: Special Markets Department, HarperCollins Publishers, Inc., 10 East 53rd Street, New York, NY 10022.

FIRST EDITION

ISBN 0-06-095151-6

02 03 04 05 RRD 15 14 13 12 11 10

Publisher: MATT GROENING
Managing Editor: JASON GRODE
Art Director - Editor: BILL MORRISON
Book Design: MARILYN FRANDSEN
Legal Guardian: SUSAN GRODE
Contributing Artists:
BILL MORRISON, TIM BAVINGTON, PHIL ORTIZ, LUIS ESCOBAR, STEPHANIE GLADDEN, STEVE VANCE, CINDY VANCE, NATHAN KANE
Contributing Writers:
BILL MORRISON, ANDREW GOTTLIEB, GARY GLASBERG, STEVE VANCE

PRINTED IN CANADA

CONTENTS

BARTMAN: AN INTRODUCTION

Once in a generation, a modest, unheralded book comes along that speaks from the heart to the deep concerns we all share about our lives. Such a book provides a beacon, a guide, a call to arms, for all who come into contact with it. Sure, it may be packaged between flimsy soft covers and filled with gaudy, colorful illustrations, but that is part of the book's unassuming message. Approaching a book like this with an open mind can only make the world seem even more miraculous, and all but the most casual reader cannot fail to be moved, changed, or filled with a new determination to live life with a heightened awareness. That is simply what happens when reading a book that is so obviously a contemporary classic. This is not that book. This is just a mess of comics. Enjoy!

MATT GROENING
Bongo Comics Group

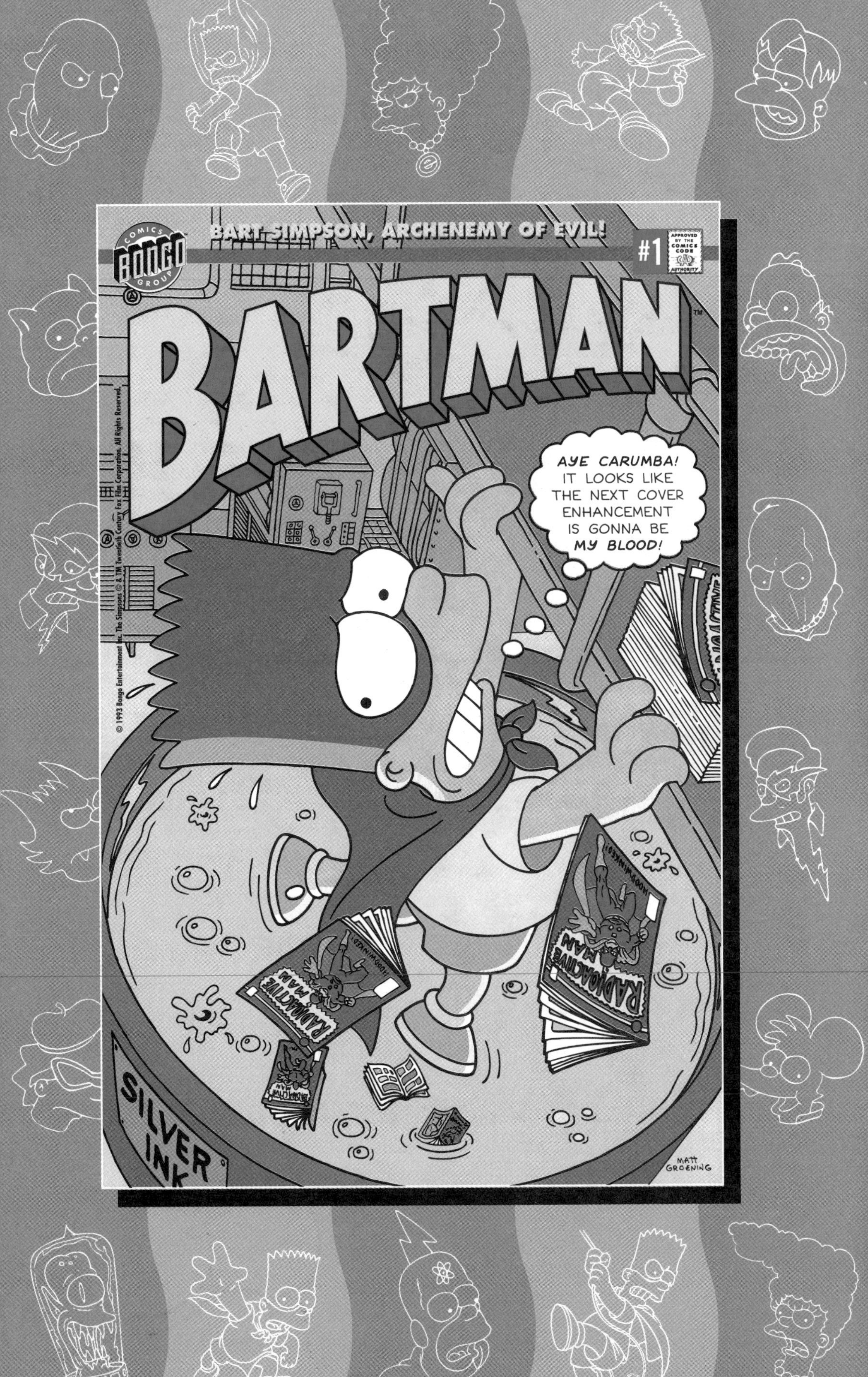
BONGO COMICS GROUP
BART SIMPSON, ARCHENEMY OF EVIL!
#1
APPROVED BY THE COMICS CODE AUTHORITY
BARTMAN™
AYE CARUMBA! IT LOOKS LIKE THE NEXT COVER ENHANCEMENT IS GONNA BE MY BLOOD!
© 1993 Bongo Entertainment Inc. The Simpsons © & TM Twentieth Century Fox Film Corporation. All Rights Reserved.
RADIOACTIVE MAN
HOODWINKED!
SILVER INK
MATT GROENING

BARTMAN'S BOTTOM 40

1. Bullies with mega-strength superpowers.
2. Parents who tell their friends about your "cute little costume."
3. School nights.
4. Learning the hard way that Man was not meant to fly.
5. Sidekicks that can't stay up past nine o'clock.
6. Using allowance to pay off anonymous tipsters.
7. Forgetting that the mobsters and the Mayor drive black limos.
8. The fine line between superhero and psycho-vigilante.
9. Sliding down the Bartpole in shorts.
10. Slick Hollywood types that try to exploit your good name.
11. The universe imploding upon itself and restarting again with subtle changes.
12. Chronic cowl-head.
13. Having homework to do before going out and bustin' heads.
14. Sharpening the giant pencil in the Bartcave.
15. Police Chiefs that only give you 24 hours to crack the case.
16. Houseboy's lactose intolerance.
17. Contracting TMJ from all that teeth gritting.
18. Psychotic villains that don't use deodorant.
19. Bartdog's bout with compulsive tail chasing.
20. The Bartcave's persistent mildew.
21. Maniac Beef Jerky Monsters from Dimension Q.
22. Getting caught soliloquizing.
23. Cape-burn.
24. Defective grappling hooks.
25. Curious sisters searching for blackmail material.
26. Comic book shops that are closed on Sunday.
27. Self-centered reporters.
28. Poorly paved streets and sidewalks.
29. Bad guys who don't use old warehouses or castles for hideouts.
30. Any use of the word "techno."
31. Senses-shattering adventures not being as senses-shattering as the good old days.
32. The obvious merchandising ploy in the "new look" Radioactive Man Adventures television show.
33. Lax security at the pen where they send costumed super-villains.
34. The criminal menace named Sideshow Bob.
35. Misjudging the distance between the window and the tree.
36. Houseboy's stash of Malibu Stacey comics.
37. A lifetime of radiation exposure, yet no cool powers.
38. "Intimidating voice" is just not intimidating.
39. Being a street fighting man in a town full of sidewalks.
40. Taking a bite out of crime and getting it stuck between your teeth.

The COMIC COVER CAPER!
NOOOO!!
A MATT GROENING PRODUCTION
SCRIPT & LAYOUTS: STEVE VANCE
PENCILS: PHIL ORTIZ
FINISHED ART: BILL MORRISON
ADDITIONAL INKS: TIM BAVINGTON
CO-PLOT & COLORS: CINDY VANCE

AN "F"?! BUT --
YES, BART. I'M AFRAID YOU DIDN'T QUITE FULFILL THE REQUIREMENTS OF THIS ASSIGNMENT.

YOUR LITTLE STORY ABOUT RADIOACTIVE MAN WAS NOT WHAT I HAD IN MIND WHEN I ASKED THE CLASS TO WRITE ABOUT "OUR FRIEND NUCLEAR ENERGY."
BUT RADIOACTIVE MAN IS THE LIVING EMBODIMENT OF THE BENEFITS OF NUCLEAR POWER! AND HE'S A FRIEND TO OPPRESSED PEOPLE EVERYWHERE!

SORRY, BART. YOU GOT AN "F" AND THAT'S FINAL -- EVEN THOUGH IT MEANS YOU'LL BE COMING BACK FOR --
SHUDDER -- SUMMER SCHOOL!

AFTER SCHOOL...
HEY, BART-DUDE! WHY SO DOWN?
MY LIFE IS RUINED, OTTO-MAN. I JUST FOUND OUT I HAVE TO GO TO SUMMER SCHOOL!

SUMMER SCHOOL? OH YEAH! I FORGOT I'M S'POSED TO DRIVE THE SCHOOL BUS THIS SUMMER!
GOOD THING YOU SAID SOMETHING -- I WAS GONNA TAKE OFF AND DRIVE A BUS FOR THE HURLING PINECONES ON THE PASTAFAZOOLA TOUR!

THAT EVENING...
GOSH, BART, I'VE NEVER SEEN YOU SO DOWNCAST. NOT EVEN THE MIRTHFUL MAYHEM OF ITCHY & SCRATCHY HAS CHEERED YOU UP.

I CAN'T HELP IT, LISA -- KNOWING THAT I HAVE TO GO TO SUMMER SCHOOL HAS TAKEN THE JOY OUT OF MY LIFE.
SLICE!
AAAIEEE
COME ON, BART, EDUCATION'S NOT THAT BAD!

BUSINESS FAT CAT
A UNITED PROLETARIAT
STRIKE
AFTER ALL, IT CAN HELP YOU APPRECIATE THE SUBTLE POLITICAL SATIRE OF ITCHY & SCRATCHY.

MAYBE YOU'RE RIGHT, LISA. I -- HEY, WAIT A MINUTE! I DON'T SEE YOU RUSHING OUT TO SIGN UP FOR SUMMER SCHOOL!
ME? GIVE UP MY SUMMER? JUST BECAUSE I'M SMART DOESN'T MEAN I'M CRAZY!

ALL TOO SOON, THE FIRST DAY OF SUMMER SCHOOL ARRIVES...
BYE! JANEY'S MOM IS DRIVING US ALL TO MT. SPLASHMORE!
HAVE FUN!
MOAN!

BART, I KNOW YOU DON'T WANT TO GO TO SCHOOL, BUT YOU'RE ONLY MAKING IT HARDER ON YOURSELF BY MOPING AROUND THIS WAY.
BESIDES, MAYBE YOU CAN REALLY LEARN SOMETHING FROM ALL THIS -- LIKE IF YOU STUDY A LITTLE HARDER, YOU WON'T HAVE TO GO NEXT SUMMER.

MOM, IT'S BAD ENOUGH THAT I HAVE TO WASTE PRECIOUS DAYS OF MY YOUTH IN SUMMER SCHOOL. DON'T MAKE IT WORSE BY ASKING ME TO ACTUALLY **LEARN** SOMETHING.
HMMM...

LATER...
MILHOUSE! ***YOU'RE*** GOING TO SUMMER SCHOOL? I THOUGHT YOU ***PASSED!***
I DID, BUT MY MOM IS SENDING ME ANYWAY. SHE SAYS HAVING ME HANGING AROUND THE HOUSE ALL SUMMER MAKES HER PLANTS DIE.

HA HA! LOOK AT THE ***LOSERS*** ON THEIR WAY TO SCHOOL!
ULP!

HA HA! ***WE*** GOT ***SUMMER JOBS,*** MAN!
YEAH, WE'RE ALMOST MAKING ***MINIMUM WAGE!***
HAVE FUN IN ***CLASS, BABIES!***
SPRINGFIEL
SCH

IF I EVER FIND OUT WHO INVENTED SUMMER SCHOOL, I'M GONNA --
ARY
GREETINGS, FELLOW SCHOLARS!

WHAT ARE ***YOU*** DOING HERE, ***BRAIN-O?*** IS YOUR MOM FORCING YOU TO GO TO SUMMER SCHOOL, TOO?
OF COURSE NOT -- I'M ATTENDING VOLUNTARILY.
HUH?!

CERTAINLY! AFTER ALL, ONE CAN'T ALLOW ONE'S MIND TO LIE FALLOW ALL SUMMER. I CRAVE THE INTELLECTUAL STIMULATION THAT ONLY YONDER HALLOWED HALLS OF LEARNING CAN PROVIDE.
POW!
I RECOGNIZE YOUR RIGHT TO REBUT MY STATEMENT, GENTLEMEN, BUT I WISH YOU HAD CHOSEN A FORM OF EXPRESSION THAT DIDN'T CAUSE **INTERNAL BLEEDING**.

GOOD MORNING, CLASS. I CAN TELL HOW **THRILLED** YOU ALL ARE TO BE HERE.
BELIEVE ME, I KNOW HOW YOU FEEL. I WOULDN'T BE HERE **MYSELF** IF I DIDN'T NEED THE MONEY.

I'D BE LYING IN THE SUN WITH A **COLD DRINK** IN ONE HAND AND A **HOT HUNK** IN THE OTHER. *SIGH*
PASSION'S TORN SHIRT
DIET COLA
SELFISH

BUT ENOUGH SELF-TORTURING DAYDREAMS. YOUR TERM PAPER TOPIC WILL BE "**THE WONDERS OF THE MARKETPLACE**."
THE WONDERS OF
TERM PAPER!? OH NO!

AFTER SCHOOL...
OOH, BABY! AFTER A HARD DAY OF SCHOOL, NOTHING HELPS YOU FORGET ALL THE JUNK THEY'VE MADE YOU LEARN LIKE A VISIT TO THE COMIC BOOK SHOP!
YES, WE'RE OPEN
507
YEAH! I HOPE THE NEW CAPTAIN SQUID CAME IN THIS WEEK!
I'M WAITING FOR THE RADIOACTIVE MAN VS. CAPTAIN SQUID CROSSOVER NEXT WEEK. WHEN THOSE TWO TITANS CLASH, IT'S SURE TO BE THE COMIC BOOK EVENT OF THE MILLENIUM OF THE MONTH! IT'S GONNA HAVE A HOLOFOIL COVER AND -- AYE CARUMBA!
NO STORY
TRADEMARK WARS
ALL PICTURE
LOCKJAW LEGION
ANGRY MAN
SNARL SQUAD
MILHOUSE, I ASK YOU -- IS THERE A MORE AWE-INSPIRING SIGHT ON GOD'S GREEN EARTH THAN AN OVERFLOWING COMIC BOOK RACK AT THE PEAK OF A SUMMER GLUT?
HOT!
PICK OF THE WEEK
MYLAR MAN
OVERLY-RENDERED MAN
Z-SCHOOL
Z-TEAM
PNEUMATICA
Z-BABIES
THE ANIMATED Z-MEN
DEATHKILL
KILLDEATH
ANOTHER BUNCH OF Z-MEN
CROSSOVER FORCE
CAPTAIN SQUID
HOLO-FOIL MAN
LEGION OF SCANTILY-CLAD SUPERHEROINES
INVESTOR
MARKET SHARE MAN
CAPTAIN STEROID
TRADING CARD COMICS
BLOODSPURT
WOW!

GREETINGS, GENTLEMEN. I SEE THAT YOU TOO HAVE STOPPED BY TO PERUSE THE LATEST INVESTMENT OPPORTUNITIES.
NAH, WE'RE JUST CHECKING OUT THE HOT NEW BOOKS.

COOL! LOOK AT THIS NEW ISSUE OF ***IRON SKULL!!*** THE COVER IS ATTACHED WITH SKULL-SHAPED RIVETS! I'VE GOTTA HAVE IT!
AND THIS ***DEATHBLOOD*** IS POLYBAGGED WITH AN INCENDIARY DEVICE THAT WILL ***DESTROY THE COMIC*** IF YOU TRY TO OPEN IT! I'M GOING TO PURCHASE AN ***EXTRA COPY!***

WE GOTTA BUY ***THIS*** BOOK -- SEE THE PEDESTRIAN IN THE BACKGROUND OF PANEL 4? THIS IS HIS FIRST APPEARANCE, AND I HEAR THEY'RE GONNA ***KILL HIM OFF*** NEXT ISSUE.
CAPTAIN COLLECTIBLE
CALLING ALL SUCKERS!
MAKE B
THEN THEY'RE GONNA ***BRING HIM BACK*** AS A ***VILLAIN*** CALLED ***THE JAYWALKER!***

HEY, ***LOOK*** -- THERE'S A COPY OF LAST MONTH'S ***CAPTAIN SQUID*** IN THE DISPLAY CASE.
ITCHY
CAPTAIN SQUID

WHOA! $50?! WHAT MAKES IT ***WORTH THAT MUCH?***
I'M ***RICH!*** I'VE GOT A COPY OF THAT ISSUE!
HY BE SKINNY?

NOT LIKE ***THIS*** YOU DON'T!
HUH? WHAT DO YOU MEAN?

OBSERVE, POINDEXTER! HERE IS AN ***ORDINARY*** COPY OF CAPTAIN SQUID #472, JUST LIKE THE ONE YOU'VE GOT. I'LL LET YOU HAVE IT FOR $2.50. NOTICE ANY DIFFERENCE BETWEEN IT AND THE ONE THAT'S GOING FOR $50?
CAPTAIN SQUID
CAPTAIN SQUID
$50
THE ONE IN THE CASE DOESN'T HAVE A ***FOIL-STAMPED LOGO!***

VERY GOOD. YOU PASS THE EYE EXAM.
BUT IF IT'S DEFECTIVE, WHY IS THE PRICE ***HIGHER?***

WHATSAMATTER? YOU NEVER HEARD OF ***SUPPLY AND DEMAND?*** OUT OF A PRINT RUN OF 500,000, ONLY ***50 COPIES*** DIDN'T GET FOIL STAMPED.
THAT MAKES 'EM ***ULTRA-RARE COLLECTOR'S ITEMS --*** HENCE THE EXORBITANT PRICE.
WOW! A ***NON-ENHANCED*** COMIC THAT'S WORTH ***MORE*** THAN AN ***ENHANCED*** COMIC! IS THAT ***LEGAL?***

I DON'T KNOW ABOUT YOU FELLOWS, BUT I'M GOING TO TAKE A SUBSTANTIAL POSITION IN ***CAPTAIN SQUIDS.*** THE MARKET INTEREST GENERATED BY THIS ERROR IS LIKELY TO SPREAD TO THE REGULAR COPIES.
MARTIN, IF THAT MEANS YOU'RE GOING TO BUY ***EXTRA COPIES,*** I'M WITH YOU.

SOON...
HEY, I JUST PUT THAT BOOK ON DISPLAY AND THE KIDS ARE DROOLING ALREADY. THEY BOUGHT OUT ***ALL*** THE ***REGULAR COPIES.***
SO -- YOU GOT ANY ***MORE*** ERROR COMICS?
JUST ***WAIT*** --
-- YOU'LL HAVE MORE SOON.

THE NEXT DAY...
TODAY YOUR SCHOOL WILL TRY TO GIVE YOU A GLIMPSE OF THE EXCITING THINGS YOU HAVE TO LOOK FORWARD TO ONCE YOU GET YOUR HIGH SCHOOL DIPLOMA.
IT'S DEAD-END CAREER DAY!

THIS AFTERNOON WE'LL BE TAKING A FIELD TRIP TO THE SPRINGFIELD PAPER AND PRINTING COMPANY.
YAWN

WE WERE GOING TO PAY A VISIT TO THE NUCLEAR POWER PLANT, BUT BECAUSE OF CERTAIN DISCIPLINE PROBLEMS WE HAD ON OUR LAST TRIP THERE, THEY ASKED US TO NEVER COME BACK.
DO NOT TOUCH THIS BUTTON
VEEP! VEEP! VEEP! VEEP!
NO!
WHOOOMPH!
SSSSSSSS!
AIEEE!!
SOMETIMES I WAKE UP IN THE MIDDLE OF THE NIGHT THINKING I HEAR THAT SIREN...

SOON...
SP&P
HOLD ONTO YOUR SEATS, KIDS! DUE TO SCHOOL BUDGET CUTBACKS, WE COULDN'T GET THE BRAKES FIXED.
SPRINGFIELD PAPER AND PRINTING CO.
"THE ANSWER TO YOUR PAPER AND PRINTING NEEDS IS CLEAR CUT."
STOP WHEN RED LIGHTS FLASH
SPRINGFIELD ELEMENTARY SCHOOL

HI THERE. I'M ***TROY MCCLURE***. YOU MAY REMEMBER ME FROM SUCH EXCITING MOTION PICTURES AS ***"CALLING ALL LUMBERJACKS"*** AND ***"THE DAY PAUL BUNYAN CRIED"*** TODAY I'LL BE TAKING YOU ON ANOTHER KIND OF ADVENTURE -- THROUGH ***THE WONDERFUL WORLD OF WOOD PULP!***

AUDITORIUM
THE COAST IS CLEAR, MAN! COME ON!

AUDITORIUM
THERE'S GOTTA BE SOMETHING FUN TO DO AROUND HERE!
YEAH -- MAYBE THERE'S A VENDING MACHINE!

AUDITORIUM
THE COAST IS CLEAR! COME ON!

I'VE GOT A MINI-BAR IN MY OFFICE. WE CAN POP OPEN A COUPLE OF DAIQUIRI MIXES AND I'LL TELL YOU HOW THE MOVIE ENDS.

MAN! TALK ABOUT DULLSVILLE! THIS IS EVEN WORSE THAN THE FIELD TRIP TO THE MUSEUM OF TWINE!
GUTENBERG BIBLES
GUTENBERG BIBLES
GUTENBERG BIBLES
GUTENBE BIBLES

WHOA! HEY, MILHOUSE -- COME HERE, MAN!

WH-WHAT IS IT, BART?
IT'S THE MOTHER LODE! LOOK!

-- THEY'RE PRINTING COMIC BOOKS!
WHEN HEROES COLLIDE!
WHEN HEROES COLLIDE!
WHEN HEROES COLLIDE!
WHEN HEROES COLLIDE!

LOOK! THOSE ARE THE INSIDE PAGES OF THE RADIOACTIVE MAN VS. CAPTAIN SQUID CROSSOVER!
I'LL BET THEY'RE GETTING READY TO PRINT THE HOLOFOIL COVERS RIGHT NOW!

WHAT DO YOU THINK YOU'RE UP TO, PUNKS?

JIMBO -- DOLPH -- KEARNY! WHAT ARE YOU GUYS DOING HERE?
WE WORK HERE.
JIMBO
DOLPH
KEARNY
ULP!

YEAH -- WE'RE PART OF THE LACKEYS OF TOMORROW TRAINING PROGRAM. SO SCRAM, SMALL FRY.
HEY, MAN -- WHAT'S THE BIG DEAL? WE WERE JUST LOOKING AROUND.

WELL, LOOK SOMEWHERE ELSE. THIS IS *OUR* TURF NOW.
BESIDES, COMIC BOOKS ARE FOR BABIES -- SO *PUSH OFF,* BABIES!
PUSH!

AND WE'D BETTER NOT CATCH YOU AROUND HERE AGAIN!
HA HA! RUN, COMIC-BOOK BABIES!
HURRY, BART -- OR WE'LL GET *WEDGIES* FOR *SURE!*

THIS IS A *WONDERFUL* IDEA...

I DON'T KNOW IF I COULD'VE SAT THROUGH THAT WHOLE FILM WITHOUT HAVING A *NERVOUS BREAKDOWN*.
I SWEAR THESE SUMMER SESSIONS SEEM TO BE GETTING *LONGER* EVERY YEAR.
CAN I FRESHEN YOUR DRINK, EDNA? THE FILM'S ONLY HALF-OVER.

WHY NOT? AT LEAST I KNOW THOSE KIDS ARE OUT OF TROUBLE FOR ANOTHER 20 MINUTES.
PLAYDUDE

LATER THAT AFTERNOON, MILHOUSE HEADS FOR THE COMIC BOOK SHOP...
MAYBE I'LL FINALLY MAKE A DEAL ON THAT ***ROLLIE FINGERS*** ROOKIE CARD TO -- ***YIKES!***
YES OPEN

IT'S ***JIMBO!***

BUT WHAT'S HE DOING AT THE COMICS SHOP? HE SAID COMICS ARE FOR BABIES! UNLESS...
...MAYBE HE COLLECTS BASEBALL CARDS!
I'M NOT GOING IN UNTIL HE LEAVES. HE MIGHT ***PUSH ME*** LIKE HE DID BART!

10 MINUTES LATER...
SEE YOU LATER, MAN.
FINALLY! HE'S LEAVING.

INSIDE THE COMICS SHOP...
SUPERIOR SQUADRON
CAPTAIN SQUID
WHOA! A ***NEW*** ERROR COMIC!
THERE'S SOMETHING STRANGE ABOUT THIS. I'D BETTER GET GOING! THIS IS A JOB FOR...

"...BARTMAN!"
SOON, A MYSTERIOUS BEACON GLOWS IN THE DARKENING SKY OVER SPRINGFIELD...
THE BARTSIGNAL! I'M NEEDED!

I HOPE BARTMAN SEES THE SIGNAL. HE...
GOOD EVENING, OLD FRIEND.

BARTMAN!
WHAT DASTARDLY EVIL STALKS SPRINGFIELD TONIGHT, MILHOUSE?

QUICKLY, MILHOUSE EXPLAINS...
HMMM... SO JIMBO WAS IN THE COMICS SHOP, EH? AND AT THE SAME TIME AS THE NEW ERROR COMIC APPEARED?
I'D BETTER INVESTIGATE FURTHER.

WHAT I DON'T UNDERSTAND IS...

ULP!
HE'S GONE!

ELSEWHERE...
KEEP YOUR EYES OPEN, MEN! WE'RE --
LOOK OUT! MORTARS!
KAWHOOMP!
YAAAAH! INCOMING!
WHAT TH--ONLY A DREAM! SOMETHING LANDED ON THE ROOF!
THOOMP!
IT'S SOME BLASTED COSTUMED VIGILANTE -- NO DOUBT TAKING THE LAW INTO HIS OWN HANDS! :SIGH: SOCIETY IS SIMPLY GOING TO HECK IN A HANDBASKET.
LET THE PROPER AUTHORITIES HANDLE IT, YOU RUFFIAN!
AHH -- THE SUPPORT OF THE PUBLIC! THAT'S WHAT MAKES A SUPERHERO'S JOB WORTHWHILE!
SOON...
ALMOST THERE! GOOD THING, TOO -- I'VE RUN OUT OF TALL THINGS TO SWING FROM!
SP&P
SPRINGFIELD PAPER AND PRINTING CO.
"THE ANSWER TO YOUR PAPER AND PRINTING NEEDS IS CLEAR CUT."

THIS END U

WHOA!

THERE THEY ARE -- THE *RADIOACTIVE MAN VS CAPTAIN SQUID* COMICS! AND THEY'VE ALREADY BEEN *FOIL-STAMPED!*
MAYBE I WAS WRONG -- IT LOOKS LIKE EVERYTHING'S OKAY!
RADIOACTIVE MAN VS. CAPTAIN SQUID
"MY CO-STAR, MY ENEMY!"

HURRY UP, MAN!
SOMEBODY'S COMING!

TIME FOR ME TO TAKE THE HIGH ROAD!

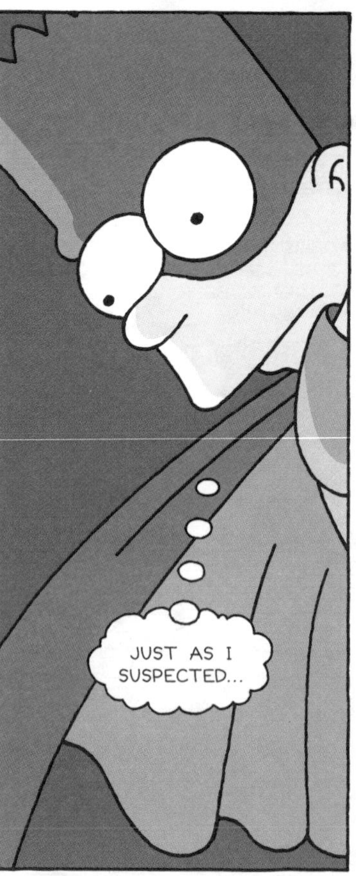
JUST AS I SUSPECTED...

...THEY'VE GOT A STACK OF COPIES THAT HAVEN'T BEEN FOIL-STAMPED!
RADIOACTIVE MAN
VS.
CAPTAIN SQUID
"MY CO-STAR MY ENEMY!"

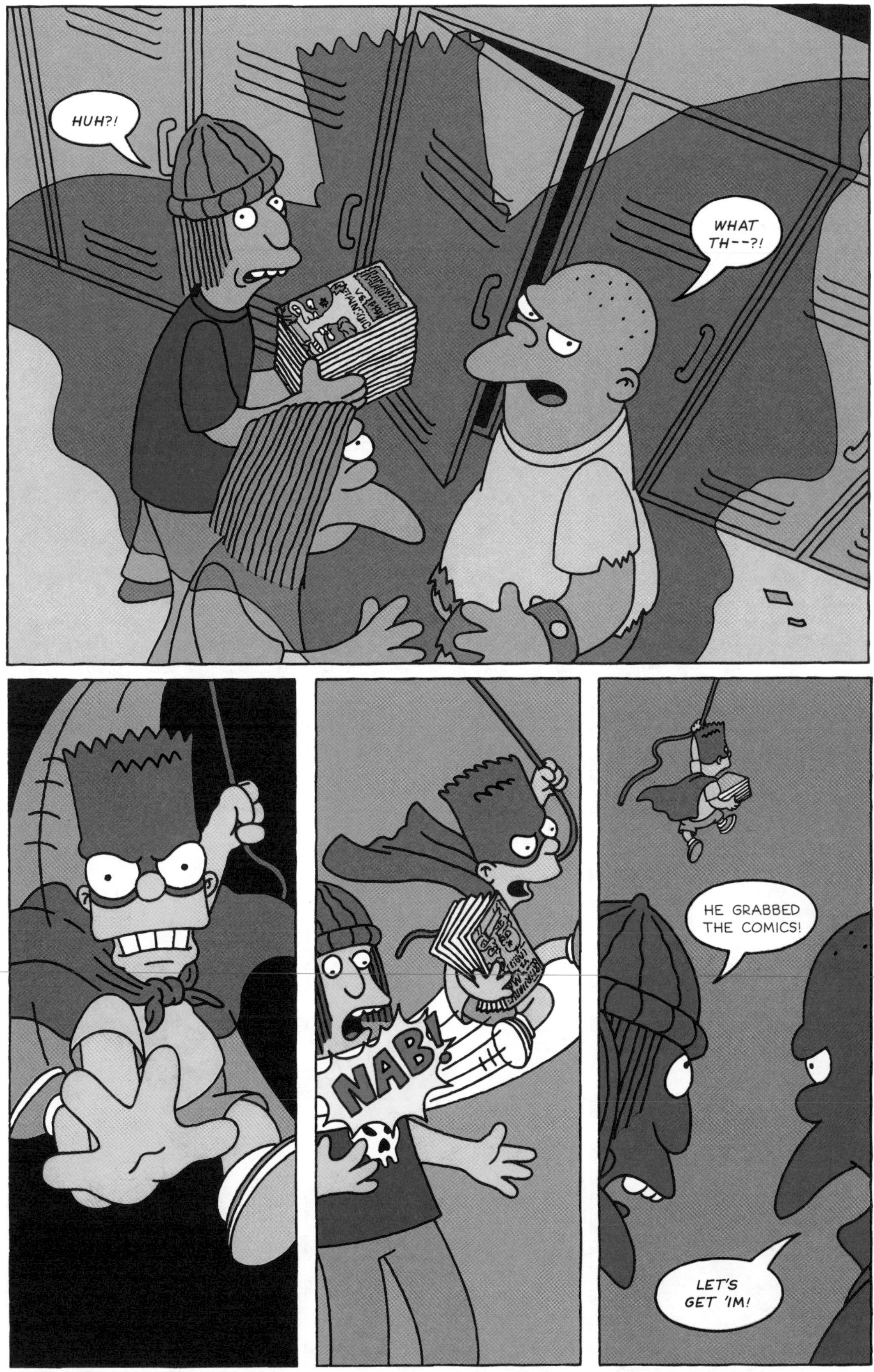

HUH?!

WHAT TH--?!

WHEW! MADE IT!
NOW IF I CAN
JUST FIND A WAY
OUT OF HERE...

HE'S UP ON
THE NEXT
LEVEL!
HURRY,
MAN! WE
CAN CUT
'IM OFF!

AYE CARUMBA!
THIS PLACE IS
A MAZE!
PLATINUM
INK
GOLD
INK

I HOPE
I'VE LOST
THOSE --
OOF!
BUMP!

FORK 'EM
OVER, MAN --
IF YOU KNOW
WHAT'S GOOD
FOR YOU!
NO WAY,
PUNK!

WAY, MAN!

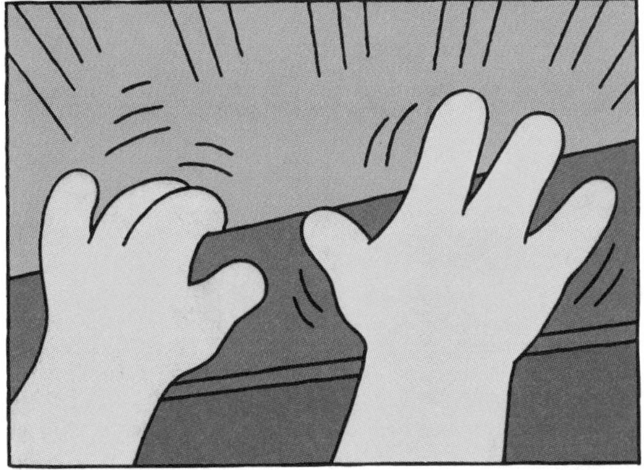

SITZER
HA HA! LOOKS LIKE YOU'RE ABOUT TO GET YOURSELF ENHANCED, CREEP!

DOES THE LITTLE BABY WANT THE COMIC BOOKS? AWW! TOO BAD!
RADIOACTIVE MAN

WHO DO YOU THINK YOU ARE, ANYWAY, DRESSED UP IN THAT STUPID COSTUME?
I'M BARTMAN --

RADIOACTIVE
SWAT!
-- AND DON'T YOU FORGET IT!

SILVER

SILVER

SILVER

SILVER

SNACKS
SILVER INK
WHA--?

HEY! MY PANTS ARE STARTING TO FALL DOWN!
HA HA!

IT'S NOT FUNNY, MAN!
HA HA!

HA H-- ULP!
SLIP!
HA HA!

IT'S NOT FUNNY, MAN!
HA H-- ULP!
SLIP!

HA HA!
SPLASH!

WELL, GUYS, IT'S BEEN FUN HANGING OUT WITH YOU, BUT I GOTTA BE ON MY WAY.
HEY! YOU CAN'T JUST LEAVE US HERE!

DON'T WORRY, MAN! I'M SURE THE GUARD WILL HAVE SYMPATHY FOR YOUR PLIGHT!
WAIT! COME BACK!

HA HA!

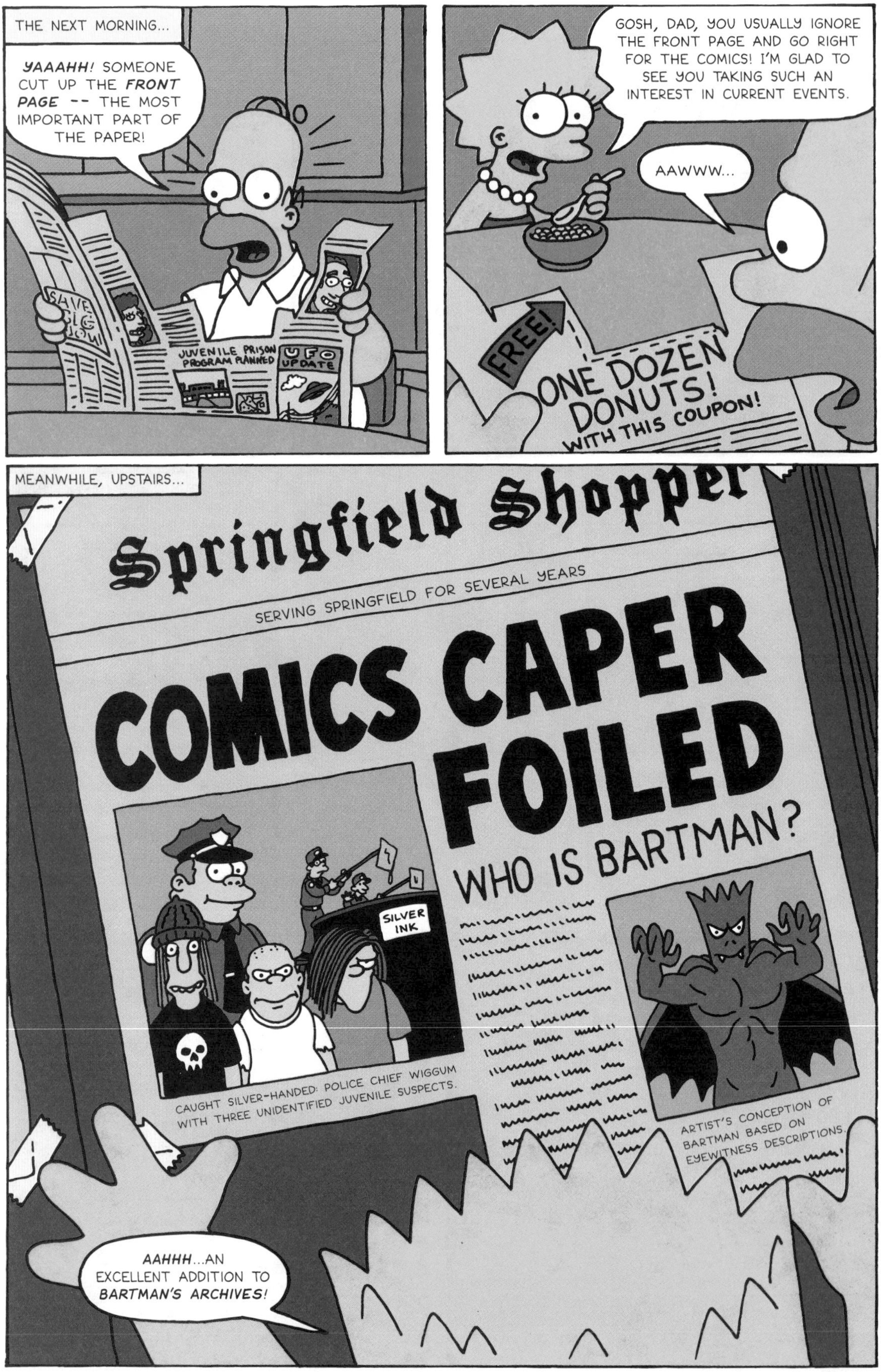

MEANWHILE, UPSTAIRS...

Springfield Shopper

SERVING SPRINGFIELD FOR SEVERAL YEARS

COMICS CAPER FOILED

WHO IS BARTMAN?

SILVER INK

CAUGHT SILVER-HANDED: POLICE CHIEF WIGGUM WITH THREE UNIDENTIFIED JUVENILE SUSPECTS.

ARTIST'S CONCEPTION OF BARTMAN BASED ON EYEWITNESS DESCRIPTIONS.

AAHHH...AN EXCELLENT ADDITION TO ***BARTMAN'S ARCHIVES***!

ELSEWHERE...
SALES ARE GREAT ON *CAPTAIN SQUID* AND *SUPERIOR SQUADRON*, BOSS -- THANKS TO THE HEAT FROM THOSE *FAKE ERROR COMICS!*
BOFFO COMICS

TOO BAD THOSE PUNKS YOU BOUGHT OFF AT THE PRINTER GOT *BUSTED* SO WE CAN'T DO ANY MORE.
Springfield Shopper
COMICS CAPER FOILED
GRRRR!

ARNOLD LEACH PUBLISHER
BEWARE, BARTMAN!
WHEN NEXT WE MEET, I SHALL HAVE MY *REVENGE!*
CRUMPLE!

LATER...
HAVE YOU FINISHED YOUR *TERM PAPER* YET?
AYE CARUMBA! I FORGOT ALL ABOUT IT! IT'S DUE *TOMORROW* -- AND I DON'T EVEN KNOW WHAT I'M GONNA WRITE ABOUT!
"TAKE ME TO YOUR COMIC BOOKS & BASEBALL CARDS!"
YES, WE'RE OPEN
GOSH, BART -- IF YOU FLUNK REGULAR SCHOOL THEY MAKE YOU GO TO SUMMER SCHOOL. WHAT DO THEY DO TO YOU IF YOU *FLUNK SUMMER SCHOOL?*

HEY, MAN -- WHAT'S THAT? ANOTHER ERROR COMIC?
NOT JUST ANOTHER ERROR COMIC -- THIS IS THE *RAREST OF THE RARE* -- AN *ALL-SILVER* COPY OF *RADIOACTIVE MAN VS. CAPTAIN SQUID!*

WOW! THE WHOLE BOOK WAS DIPPED IN SILVER INK!
BUT THE PAGES ARE ALL STUCK TOGETHER! YOU CAN'T READ IT!

THAT IS PRECISELY THE POINT! SINCE IT CANNOT BE READ, IT WILL STAY IN MINT CONDITION FOREVER!
WOW!
YOINK!

AND SINCE THERE ARE ONLY 6 COPIES IN EXISTENCE, THE PRICE IS PROPORTIONATELY HIGHER.
$200?!
SUPERIOR SQUADRON
SQUID
$200

A FEW DAYS LATER...
GOOD MORNING, CLASS. I HAVE YOUR PAPERS ON THE WONDERS OF THE MARKETPLACE GRADED AND READY TO GIVE BACK TO YOU.

WELL DONE, BART. OF COURSE, I HAD TO DEDUCT FOR SPELLING, GRAMMAR, AND LOWBROW SUBJECT MATTER, BUT YOUR GRASP OF THE CONCEPT WAS REMARKABLY CLEAR. I APPRECIATE YOU TAKING THE ASSIGNMENT SERIOUSLY.
DON'T THANK ME, THANK BARTMAN!
C+
SUPPLY AND DEMAND IN THE COMIC BOOK MARKET BY BART SIMPSON
THE END

COMICS BONGO GROUP
BART SIMPSON, ARCHENEMY OF EVIL!
#2
APPROVED BY THE COMICS CODE AUTHORITY
BARTMAN™
© 1994 BONGO ENTERTAINMENT, INC. THE SIMPSONS © & TM TWENTIETH CENTURY FOX FILM CORPORATION. ALL RIGHTS RESERVED.
MATT GROENING
S. VANCE
Morrison

THIS IS NOT AN ADVERTISEMENT

HEY, KIDS! HAVE YOUR TASTE BUDS BEEN KRUSTIFIED YET?

If not, bug your mom 'til she buys you...

Make it a Komplete Krusty breakfast with a heaping plateful of

OFFICIAL KRUSTY BRAND PORK PRODUCTS

"Accept no imitations—except KRUSTY Brand Imitation Pork Products"

WHERE STALKS...
THE PENALIZER!
AN EVIL PRESENCE PROWLS SPRINGFIELD THIS NIGHT -- AND IT'S UP TO BARTMAN TO STOP HIM!
SPRINGFIELD SHOPS
MORTELLA BILLBOARDS
A MATT GROENING PRODUCTION
JAN STRNAD SCRIPT
STEVE VANCE PENCILS, EDITS
BILL MORRISON ☆ TIM BAVINGTON ☆ PHIL ORTIZ FINISHED ART
CINDY VANCE COLORS, EDITS

...BUT HE'D BETTER SHOW UP SOON OR I'M GOING HOME! ITCHY & SCRATCHY ARE ON IN 15 MINUTES!
KWIK -E- MART
IT IS SUCH A SHAME TO DISCARD PICKLED EGGS WHEN THEY ARE ONLY SLIGHTLY CONTAMINATED...
KWIK-E-MART
NO DUMPING

...BUT SINCE THEY HAVE BEGUN TO MUTATE, SALES HAVE DROPPED PRECIPITOUSLY!

:SIGH: UNSOLD PRODUCT IS THE SECRET SHAME OF THE KWIK-E-MART CLERK.
PICKLED EGGS
SKURGLE
10 GALLONS SQUISHEE SYRUP
GRAY FLAVOR
SPRINGFIELD MONORAIL SOUVENIR T-SHIRTS

IN ORDER TO PREVENT A RECURRENCE OF THIS UNFORTUNATE INCIDENT, PERHAPS THIS TIME I SHOULD RINSE THE CONTAINER BEFORE REFILLING IT!

SLAM!
KLIK! KLAK! LOCK! BOLT! CLUNK!
CLATTA! CLATTA!

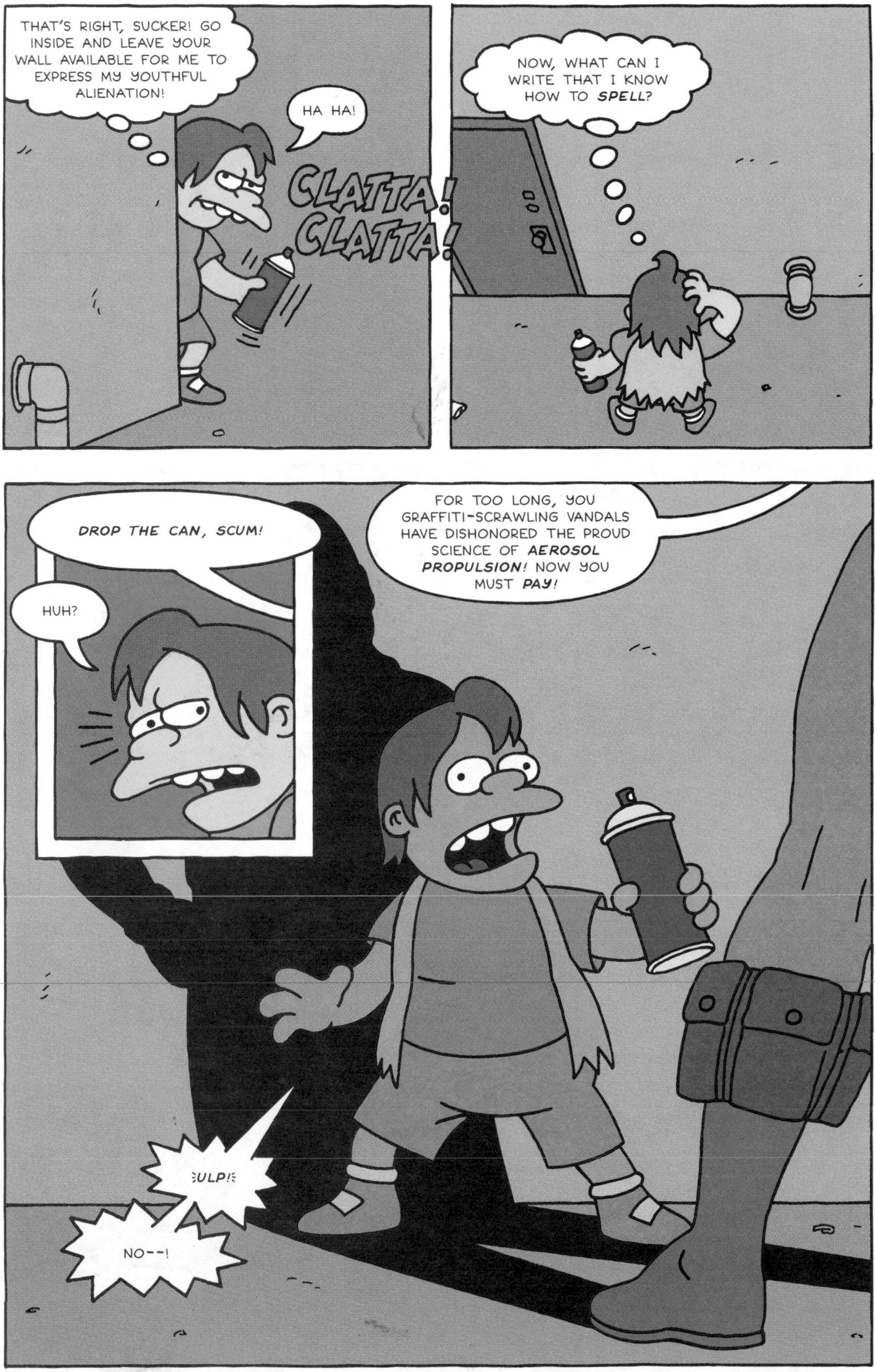

DROP THE CAN, SCUM!
FOR TOO LONG, YOU GRAFFITI-SCRAWLING VANDALS HAVE DISHONORED THE PROUD SCIENCE OF AEROSOL PROPULSION! NOW YOU MUST PAY!
HUH?
GULP!
NO--!

LATER...
IT'S BEEN A QUIET NIGHT. PERHAPS MY QUARRY HAS LEFT SPRINGFIELD FOR GREENER PASTURES.

:GASP: OR MAYBE NOT!
LOOKS LIKE I'M GONNA MISS ITCHY & SCRATCHY AFTER ALL! GOOD THING IT'S A RERUN!

IT'S NELSON -- IN SOME KIND OF A TRANCE! I'M TOO LATE...
EL BAR

...THAT FIEND HAS STRUCK AGAIN!
I WILL NOT DEFACE PRIVATE PROPERTY

NELSON! SNAP OUT OF IT! WHO DID THIS TO YOU?!
...AS IF I DIDN'T ALREADY KNOW!
UNNHH...
SMEK!

AAAAHHH!!

IT WAS...
HIM!
YOU MEAN...
YEAH... IT WAS...

...THE PENALIZER!
WHO IS THIS MYSTERIOUS FIGURE WHO STALKS SPRINGFIELD'S STREETS, METING OUT HARSH PUNISHMENT TO OUR CITY'S SCOFFLAWS?

TUNE IN LATER FOR OUR SPECIAL REPORT: THE PENALIZER -- DANGEROUS LUNATIC OR MENACING WACKO? TONIGHT ON THE SIX O'CLOCK NEWS!

TAP TAP TAP

HUH?
WHAT? IT IS?
OH.

WELL, HERE'S THE REPORT, THEN.

IF YOU ASK ME, THIS PENALIZER GUY'S DOING US ALL A BIG FAVOR! EVEN THE SMALLEST CRIMES SHOULD BE PUNISHED!
PROPERTY MOE'S TAVERN
PROPERTY OF SPRINGFIELD NUCLEAR POWER PLANT
PROPERTY OF BARNEY'S BOWL-O-RAMA

HMMM...I DON'T KNOW, HOMEY -- IT ISN'T THE PLACE OF PRIVATE CITIZENS TO TAKE THE LAW INTO THEIR OWN HANDS!

MOM FEELS SO STRONGLY ABOUT IT -- I DARE NOT TELL HER THAT I AM THE RENEGADE CRIMEFIGHTER BARTMAN!

I'M HERE AT THE SPRINGFIELD HOSPITAL WITH **DR. JULIUS HIBBERT,** THE MAN IN CHARGE OF **TREATING** THE **PENALIZER'S GROWING LIST OF VICTIMS!**
HELLO, KENT.
SPECIAL REPORT

DOCTOR, HOW HAVE THE ACTIVITIES OF THIS BIZARRE VIGILANTE IMPACTED THE HOSPITAL?
IN ORDER TO TREAT THIS NEW WAVE OF PATIENTS, WE'VE HAD TO RE-OPEN THE HOSPITAL'S **WEST WING!** WE HAVEN'T NEEDED THAT EXTRA SPACE SINCE THAT, ER..."INCIDENT" AT THE NUCLEAR POWER PLANT.

YES, I'M SURE ALL OUR VIEWERS REMEMBER THAT, ER..."INCIDENT."
CURSE THE IRRESPONSIBLE MEDIA! SMITHERS, IF THEY EVER RUN THAT **TAPE AGAIN,** SEE THAT THEIR POWER IS **CUT OFF!**
FILE TAPE
WITH PLEASURE, SIR!

HOW ABOUT YOU OLD-TIMER? WERE YOU ASSAULTED BY **THE PENALIZER?**
NO! A **MUTANT EGG** BIT ME ON THE BACKSIDE!

IT WAS GREEN AND SLIMY AND HAD **SHARP TEETH**...
THE PENALIZER'S VICTIMS ARE **IN HERE,** KENT. I WARN YOU -- IT'S **NOT A PRETTY SIGHT!**
WEST WING

I'M AN EXPERIENCED REPORTER, DOCTOR. I'VE SEEN THINGS THAT WOULD TURN YOUR HAIR WH-- ;GASP;

YES, THE SPECTACLE OF ALL THESE UNFORTUNATES IS RATHER SHOCKING, ISN'T IT? FOR INSTANCE, THIS TEENAGER, AN ADMITTED **LOITERER,** WAS FORCED TO STAND WITH HIS NOSE AGAINST THE WALL FOR **TWELVE HOURS!**
ID WUD DE MOST HORRIBUH NIGHT OB MY LIFE!
TERRIBLE!

THESE PATIENTS, CAUGHT **MAKING FACES** OUT THE WINDOW OF A CITY BUS, MAY WEAR THOSE EXPRESSIONS FOR THE REST OF THEIR LIVES!
TRAGIC! AND AT SUCH A **TENDER AGE!**

THEY ALL HAD IT COMING!
DAD! A LITTLE HUMAN COMPASSION FOR THESE HAPLESS MISCREANTS WOULD NOT BE INAPPROPRIATE!
PROPERTY OF

SEE MARGE?! LISA **AGREES** WITH ME!
HRRMMMM...

...AND HERE, THE PENALIZER HAS SOMEHOW MENTALLY COMPELLED THIS MAN TO PERFORM **20,000 JUMPING JACKS!**
AND WHAT WAS **HIS ALLEGED OFFENSE?**
...18,264, 18,265...
HE WAS CAUGHT BELCHING EXCESSIVELY OUTSIDE OF MOE'S BAR!
YAAAAAH!

THIS MADMAN HAS GONE TOO FAR! THE PENALIZER MUST BE **STOPPED!**

STRANGE -- IT ISN'T LIKE BART TO LET THIS KIND OF FAMILY DISCUSSION PASS WITHOUT SARCASTIC COMMENT. I WONDER IF HE'S SICK OR SOMETHING.
SOMETHING ABOUT THE PENALIZER'S **MODUS OPERANDI** IS DISTURBINGLY FAMILIAR -- BUT WHAT IS IT?
WHAT?
WHAT?
OH, LOOK -- THERE'S **POLICE CHIEF WIGGUM!** IT'S REASSURING TO SEE OUR TOWN'S TOP LAW-ENFORCEMENT OFFICER ON THE CASE!
CAN YOU TAKE THE TIME TO HAVE A WORD WITH US, CHIEF?
WHA -- ? OH, HELLO, KENT. I WAS JUST, UH, TAKING A LITTLE **BREAK** FROM OUR **GRUELING INVESTIGATION!** MAN, THIS CASE IS **TOUGH!**
FOR THE LAST TIME -- CLEAN UP YOUR OWN MESS, YOU PIGS!
WHAT WILL YOUR NEXT STEP BE?
I'M ABOUT TO QUESTION A BUNCH OF PEOPLE **THE PENALIZER** CAUGHT **CUTTING IN LINE** AT A MOVIE THEATER. HE MADE IT **PRETTY UGLY** FOR THEM! YOU WANNA WATCH?
N-NO MORE, PLEASE. I-I'VE SEEN **ENOUGH!**
ONE LAST QUESTION, CHIEF -- HOW DOES THE PENALIZER FORCE HIS VICTIMS TO **OBEY** HIS **SINISTER COMMANDS**?
WELL, KENT, ALONG WITH **WHO** THE PENALIZER IS, WHAT HE **LOOKS LIKE,** AND **WHY** HE'S DOING THIS, THAT'S THE **ONE QUESTION** WE HAVEN'T BEEN ABLE TO ANSWER!

THE NEXT DAY...
GOOD MORNING, MS. KRABAPPEL!
WHAT BRINGS YOU HERE, PRINCIPAL SKINNER -- ANOTHER SURPRISE VISIT FROM SUPERINTENDENT CHALMERS?
UH-OH!

I WANT YOU TO SEND...
...*THIS PERSON*...
...TO MY OFFICE RIGHT AWAY!

CARRY ON, MS. K. -- AND SEE THAT I'M NOT KEPT WAITING!
POMPOUS JERK!

:SIGH: OFF TO THE PRINCIPAL'S OFFICE AGAIN -- AND I HAVEN'T EVEN HAD TIME TO *DO ANYTHING BAD* TODAY!

WHERE ARE YOU GOING, BART? I HAVEN'T READ THE NAME ON THIS SLIP OF PAPER YET!
YOU MEAN, FOR ONCE, IT *ISN'T ME*?

HMMM...
NO, IT'S YOU. TOO BAD.
SEND ME THE BOY

MOMENTS LATER...
GULP! JIMBO, DOLPH, KEARNY, AND NELSON ARE HERE! WHATEVER'S GOING ON MUST BE BIG!
BART, I'M SURE YOU KNOW WHY I'VE CALLED YOU HERE TODAY.
S. SKINNER
THE LAB FROGS. THE RESTROOM INCIDENT. NO, THE STINK BOMBS -- DEFINITELY THE STINK BOMBS.
I CAN'T IMAGINE, SIR.

SURELY YOU NOTICED THE CONDITION OF OUR SCHOOL FLAG WHEN YOU ARRIVED THIS MORNING!
WE HAVE A SCHOOL FLAG?

SOMEONE HAS DESECRATED OUR SACRED BANNER!
NGFIELD
MENTARY

AS YOU CAN SEE FROM THIS ILLUSTRATION OF THE INTACT BANNER BY ONE OF OUR GRADUATES, THE EMBLEM OF OUR MASCOT, THE SPRINGFIELD ELEMENTARY PUMA, IS NOW MISSING! SOMEONE CUT IT OUT!
SPRIGFƎILD
ELMENTRY
S. SKINNER
HONEST, SIR -- I DON'T KNOW ANYTHING ABOUT IT!

I EXPECTED YOU TO DENY YOUR GUILT -- YOUR KIND ALWAYS DOES!
THE 'NAM WAS FULL OF NE'ER-DO-WELLS LIKE YOU!
CONSCIENTIOUS OBJECTORS -- FRAGGERS -- DESERTERS -- WHINERS AND SLACKERS!
YES, I KNOW YOUR KIND -- I KNOW THEM WELL!

YOU WON'T GET AWAY WITH THIS OUTRAGE, PRIVATE SIMPSON!
HUH?

IF THAT FLAG ISN'T REPAIRED BY 0900 HOURS TOMORROW, I'LL COURT MARTIAL THE LOT OF YOU! DISMISSED!

SLAM!
AYE CARUMBA! SKINNER'S GONE OVER FLASHBACK FALLS WITHOUT A BARREL!
SEYMOUR SKINNER
PRINCIPAL
AS IF I DIDN'T HAVE ENOUGH TO WORRY ABOUT WITH THE PENALIZER ON THE LOOSE!

LATER...
...NEW INTERVIEWS WITH SEVERAL OF THE PENALIZER'S VICTIMS REVEALED STARTLING NEW FACTS ABOUT JUST WHO OR WHAT THIS STRANGE CREATURE OF THE NIGHT MAY BE!
?
THE PENALIZER

THERE WAS THIS GIANT EYEBALL, AND IT, LIKE, HYPNOTIZED ME!

I SAW A BEER CAN -- AN' IT WAS TALKING TO ME! ⁝BELCH⁝

I REMEMBER THE FANGS COMING FOR ME, GETTING READY TO TEAR ME TO SHREDS!

"AS YOU CAN SEE, THIS STRANGE FIGURE SKULKING ON A ROOFTOP IN THE BACKGROUND BEARS AN, ER, UNCANNY RESEMBLANCE TO OUR OWN COMPUTERIZED COMPOSITE, RIGHT DOWN TO THE, UH, NUMBER OF LIMBS..."

12:00
SUN

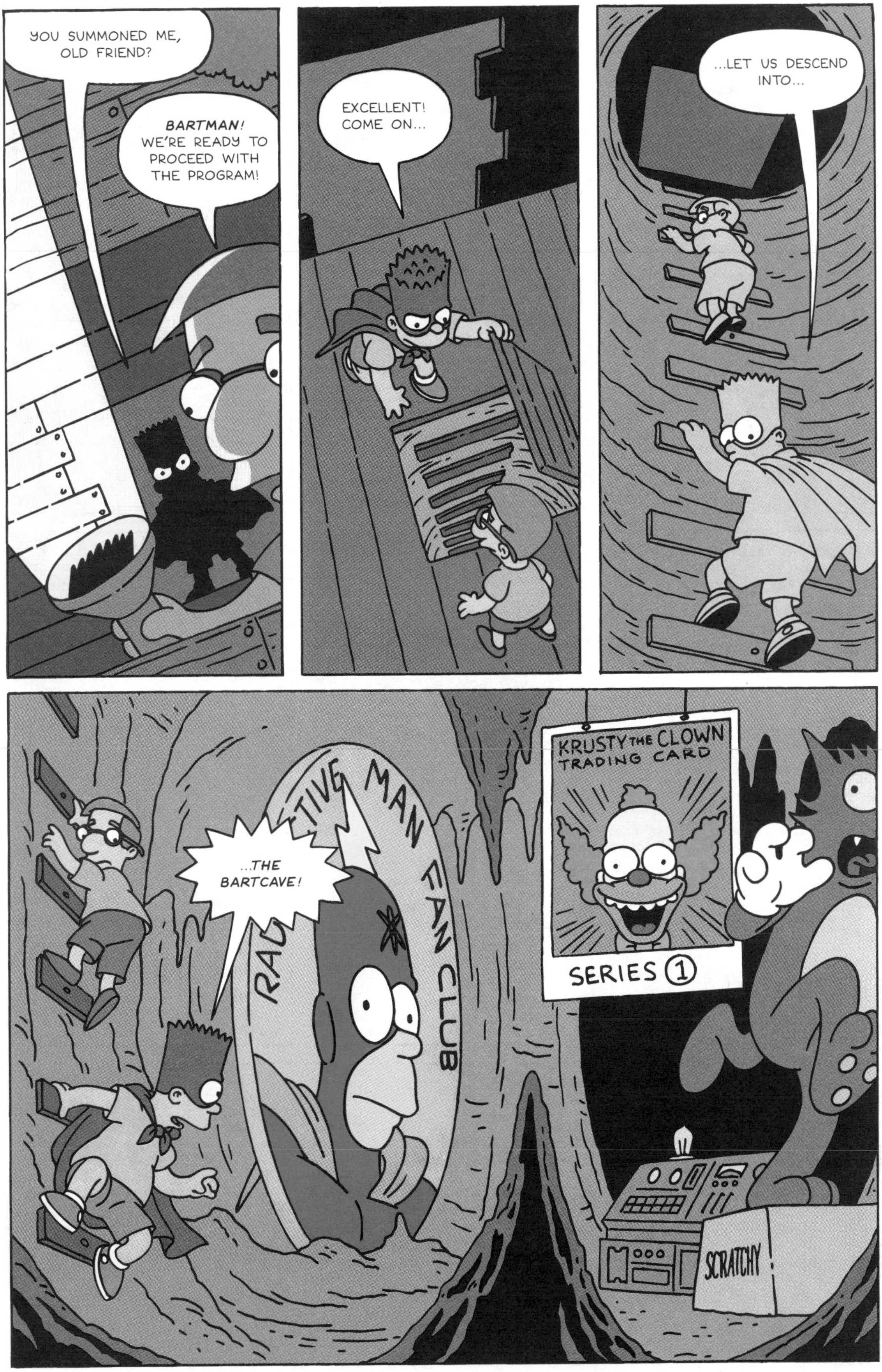

...THE BARTCAVE!

KRUSTY THE CLOWN TRADING CARD

SERIES 1

SCRATCHY

REMEMBER THE OLD DAYS, BEFORE WE DISCOVERED THE BARTCAVE?
YEAH -- WHEN WE HAD TO HIDE ALL THE MEMENTOS OF YOUR ADVENTURES IN YOUR BEDROOM!

IF IT :OOF: WON'T FIT UNDER THE BED, WE'LL :PANT: HANG IT FROM THE :UNNHH: CEILING...
SERIES 1
KRUSTY THE CLOWN TRADING CARD
:HUFF: RIGHT. :PUFF:

I'VE ENTERED THE COORDINATES OF ALL OF THE PENALIZER'S KNOWN APPEARANCES INTO THE BARTCOMPUTER!
GOOD! NOW WE'LL HAVE THE MACHINE ANALYZE THE INFO AND SEE IF IT CAN DETECT A PATTERN!

LOOK AT ALL THOSE FLASHING LIGHTS! BOY, THIS NEW COMPUTER IS GREAT!
YEAH -- THANKS TO THE DEFENSE DEPARTMENT BUILD-DOWN, YOU CAN GET ALL KINDS OF COOL STUFF FROM THOSE ADS IN THE BACK OF COMIC BOOKS!
KLIK
WHIRRR

TEN MINUTES LATER...
AHA! ALL THE ATTACKS CENTER ON ONE PLACE -- SPRINGFIELD ELEMENTARY!
GOSH, WITHOUT THE BARTCOMPUTER IT WOULD'VE TAKEN US 15 MINUTES AND A DOZEN MAP TACKS TO FIGURE THAT OUT!

BUT THAT STILL DOESN'T TELL US WHO THE PENALIZER IS, BARTMAN!
BARTMAN?
HE'S...GONE! HOW DOES HE DO THAT?!

FIRST STOP, SPRINGFIELD ELEMENTARY!
NOT ONLY DO I KNOW WHO THE PENALIZER IS, BUT I HAVE A STRONG HUNCH ABOUT HOW HE CONTROLS HIS VICTIMS!

SEYMOUR SKINNER PRINCIPAL
IF MY HUNCH IS RIGHT, THE PENALIZER HAS GOTTEN HIS HANDS ON ONE OF THE MOST FRIGHTFUL WEAPONS OF THE MODERN WORLD!

PRINCIPAL SKINNER KEEPS THE MOST DANGEROUS ITEMS HE'S CONFISCATED FROM STUDENTS IN THIS SAFE! I'LL SOON KNOW IF...

JUST AS I FEARED -- IT'S GONE!
HUCKLEBERRY FINN

GOT YE! IT'S THE MOORS FOR YOU, LADDIE!
GROUNDS-KEEPER WILLIE -- YOU DON'T UNDERSTAND! SOMEONE'S STOLEN...
...THE HYPNO-COIN!

BY THE BONNIE BANKS O' LOCH LOMOND! YER RIGHT!
ACH! WELL DO I REMEMBER THAT CURSED OBJECT --

"-- AND TH' UNKNOWN BLA'GUARD WHO WIELDED IT!"
ON MY COMMAND, YOU WILL ALL BECOME CHICKENS! ON MY COMMAND...

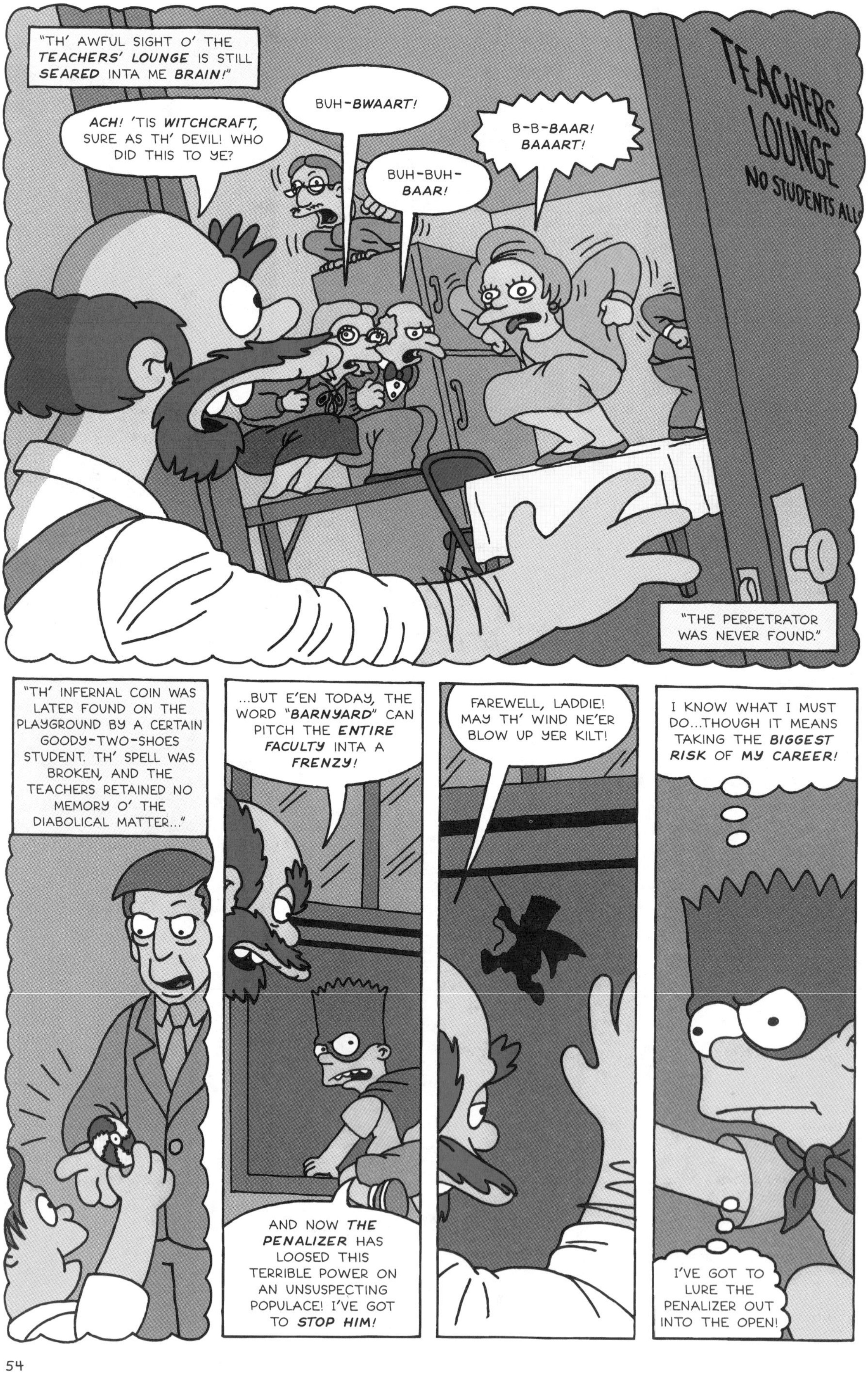

"TH' AWFUL SIGHT O' THE **TEACHERS' LOUNGE** IS STILL **SEARED** INTA ME **BRAIN**!"

ACH! 'TIS **WITCHCRAFT**, SURE AS TH' DEVIL! WHO DID THIS TO YE?

BUH-**BWAART**!

BUH-BUH-**BAAR**!

B-B-**BAAR**! **BAAART**!

TEACHERS LOUNGE NO STUDENTS ALL

"THE PERPETRATOR WAS NEVER FOUND."

SOON...
THE ENEMIES OF ORDER SEEK TO CONCEAL THEMSELVES IN THE SHADOWS OF NIGHT...
...BUT THEY CANNOT HIDE FROM THE UNBLINKING EYE OF FANATICISM!

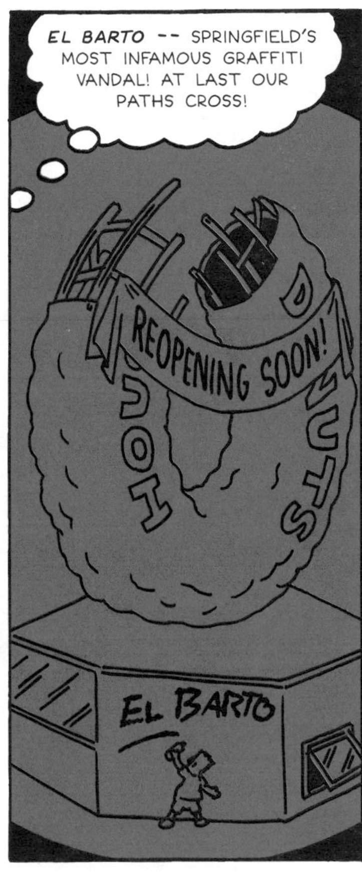
EL BARTO -- SPRINGFIELD'S MOST INFAMOUS GRAFFITI VANDAL! AT LAST OUR PATHS CROSS!
REOPENING SOON!
DONUTS
EL BARTO

SO, BART SIMPSON -- YOU ARE EL BARTO! I NEVER WOULD HAVE GUESSED!
GULP! THE PENALIZER!

YOU DID IT -- I SAW YOU DO IT -- I CAN PROVE EVERYTHING!
THIS GUY'S FAST! HE'S ANTICIPATING MY REPARTEE!

HOW IRONIC THAT YOUR UNDER-ACHIEVING WAYS WILL BE ENDED BY A DEVICE CONFISCATED FROM SOME UNKNOWN UNDERACHIEVER! YOU ARE HELPLESS BEFORE THE AWESOME POWER OF THE HYPNO-COIN!
AT MY COMMAND, YOU WILL BECOME A MODEL STUDENT!

YOU WANT TO JOIN THE CHESS CLUB! YOU WILL DEMAND MORE HOMEWORK!
MUSTN'T... LOOK AT... COIN!
GOT TO... GET AWAY...

HIDING IN THE BASEMENT WON'T HELP YOU, SIMPSON -- I'LL PURSUE YOU TO THE ENDS OF THE EARTH!
THAT'S WHAT I'M COUNTING ON!

SUDDENLY...
HOLD IT, YOU!
BLAM! BLAM!
WHAT TH--?! THE POLICE!

WUDDA WUDDA WUDDA
THERE'S NO ESCAPE! SURRENDER TO THE OFFICER!
THEY'RE EVERYWHERE! I NEVER DREAMED THEY WERE CLEVER ENOUGH TO CATCH ME!

HALT!
BLASTED MUTANT EGG! SLIPPED RIGHT OUTTA THE HANDCUFFS!
EL BARTO
BLAM!

HA! INCOMPETENT BUNGLERS! THEY'LL NEVER KNOW HOW CLOSE THEY CAME! NOW TO DEAL WITH...
BLAM! BLAM! BLAM!

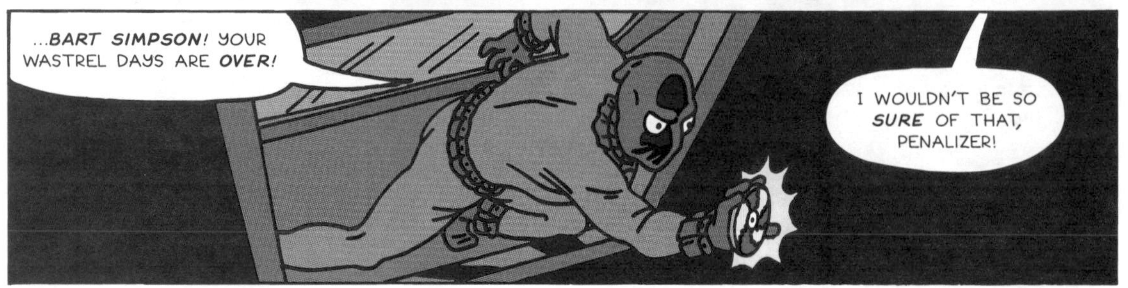
...BART SIMPSON! YOUR WASTREL DAYS ARE OVER!
I WOULDN'T BE SO SURE OF THAT, PENALIZER!

WARNING!
BATTER UNDER
HIGH PRESSURE
SPAK!

LET'S SEE HOW GOOD YOU ARE WITHOUT THAT MAIL-ORDER MENACE!
BARTMAN! SO THIS WAS ALL A RUSE!
YES! YOUNG BART SIMPSON MERELY POSED AS EL BARTO TO LEAD YOU TO ME!

WRONG! HE HAS LED ME TO YOU!
ISN'T THAT WHAT I SAID?

IF I CAN JUST FIND THE HYPNO-COIN, I CAN USE HIS OWN WEAPON AGAINST HIM!

UHHHNN! I'M HIT!

THAT'S ONLY A TASTE OF WHAT'S IN STORE FOR YOU, BARTMAN!
STRAWBER
JELLY
YIKES! A HIGH-PRESSURE JELLY GUN!

SPLAT!
SPLAT!
X-LARG
SPRINKLES
50 LBS.
SPLAT!

TRY CHEWING ON THESE, PENALIZER!

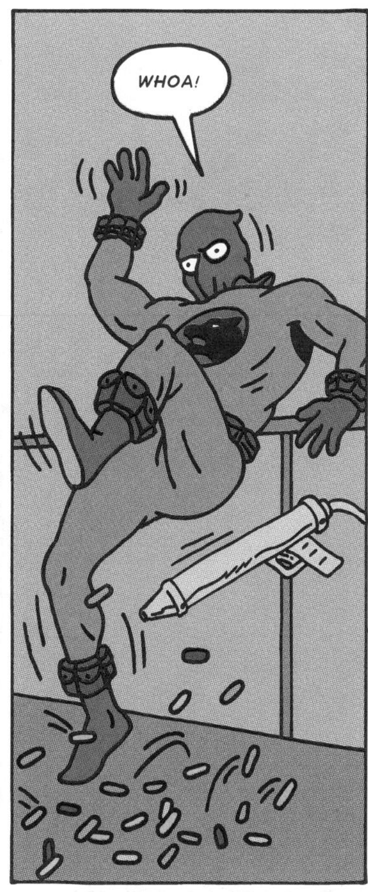
WHOA!

WHUMPF
FLOUR
FLOUR

OH, NO! THE HYPNO-COIN!
FLOUR
FLOUR
FLOUR

IF THE PENALIZER SEES IT...
THE HYPNO-COIN!
FLOUR

I'LL NEVER REACH THE COIN BEFORE THE PENALIZER DOES! ONLY ONE CHANCE...!

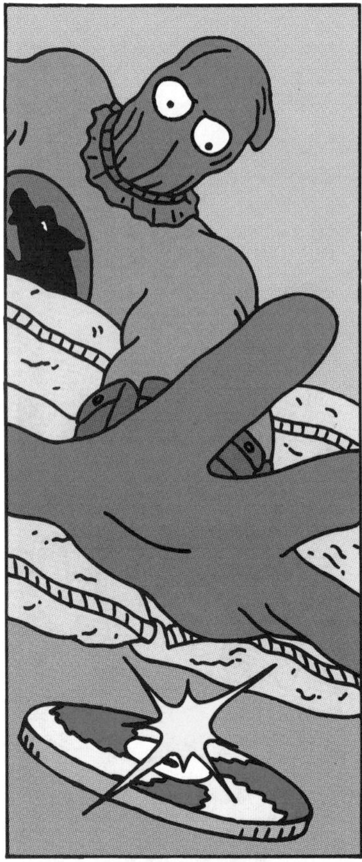

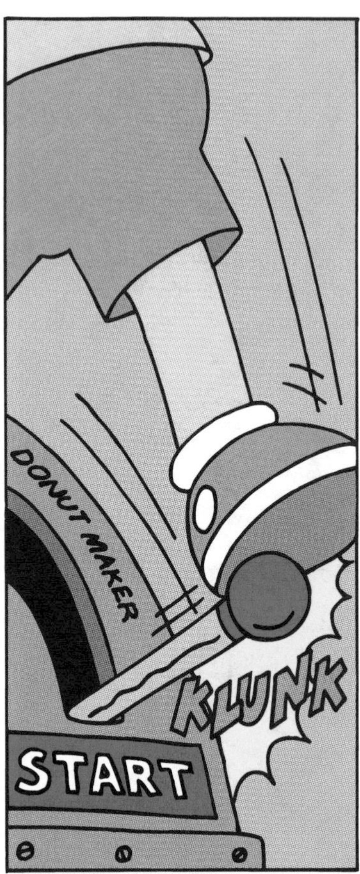
DONUT MAKER
KLUNK
START

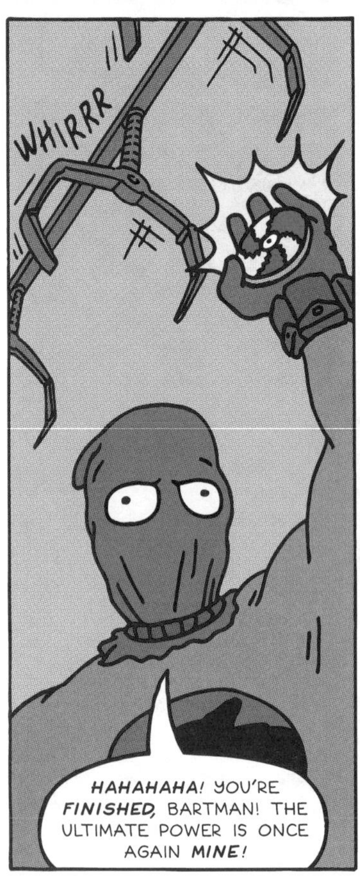
WHIRRR
HAHAHAHA! YOU'RE FINISHED, BARTMAN! THE ULTIMATE POWER IS ONCE AGAIN MINE!

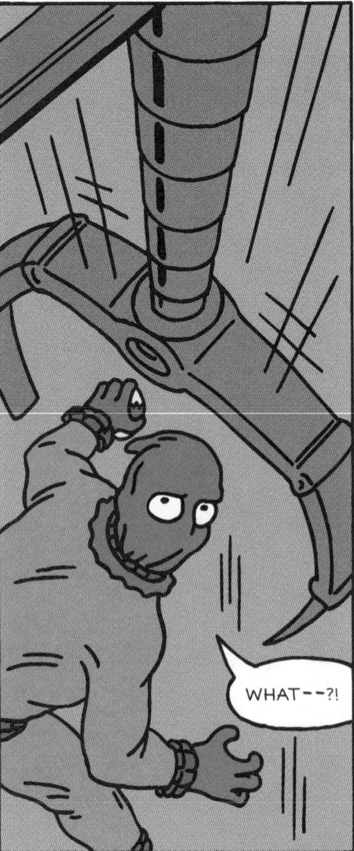
WHAT--?!

BARTMAN -- NO!
NAB!
FLOUR
KLIK

BARTMAN...**HELP!** I'LL **GIVE YOU** THE **COIN** -- JUST **SAVE ME! PLEASE!**
KLIK
CHURNK CHURNK CHURNK
SPLOOSH!
FLOUR

LEVER...**STUCK! WON'T...BUDGE!**
START

TAKE THE COIN! IT'S **YOURS!** JUST STOP THIS INFERNAL **MACHINE!**
CHURNK CHURNK CHURNK

KLIK!
NOOOOOOO!
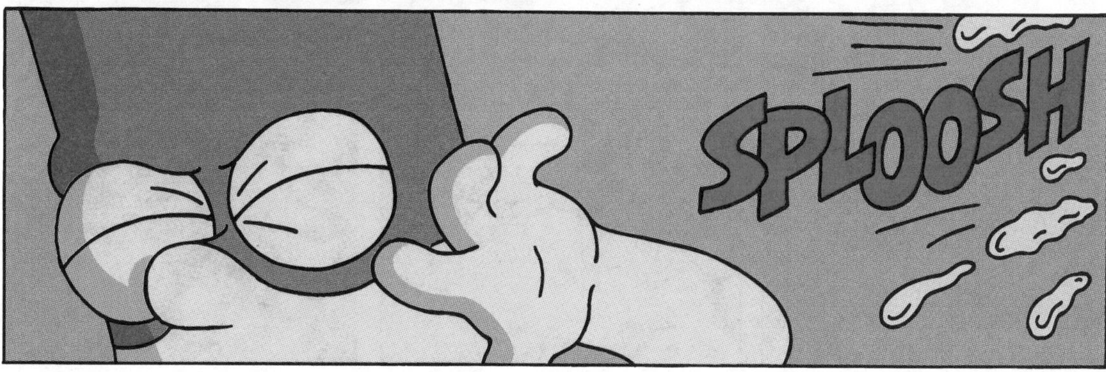
SPLOOSH

I NEVER MEANT IT TO END...LIKE *THIS!* ≷CHOKE≷
PLOP!

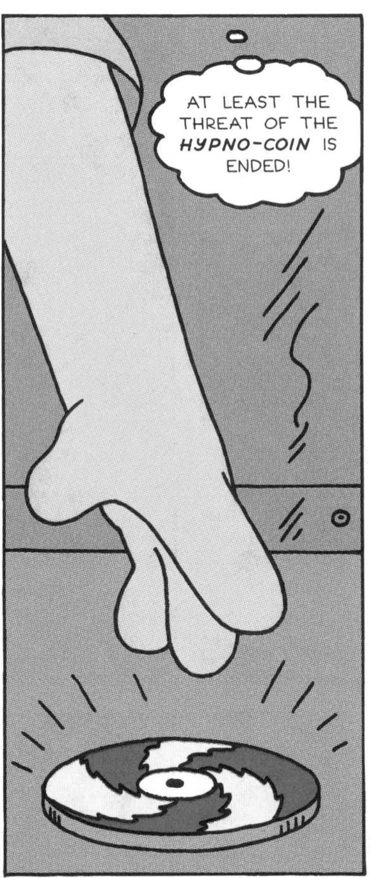
AT LEAST THE THREAT OF THE *HYPNO-COIN* IS ENDED!

ALL ITS POWER COULDN'T SAVE THE PENALIZER FROM BECOMING *DONUT BATTER!* THOUGH I CAN'T HELP THINKING...
PLOP PLOP PLOP

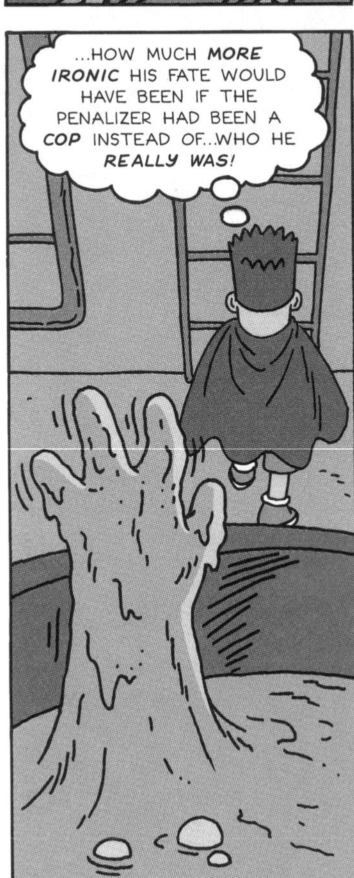
...HOW MUCH *MORE IRONIC* HIS FATE WOULD HAVE BEEN IF THE PENALIZER HAD BEEN A *COP* INSTEAD OF...WHO HE *REALLY WAS!*

BWARRL!

AAAAAAGH!
D NUTS
HOU,

BARTMAN'S BEEN GONE FOR **HOURS!** I HOPE HE'S ALL RIGHT!
⁝SIGH⁝ THESE LONELY VIGILS ARE THE HARDEST PART OF BEING A **SIDEKICK!**

BARTMAN! YOU'RE **BACK!**
I AM WEARY, MY FRIEND!

WHAT HAPPENED? DID YOU CATCH **THE PENALIZER?**
THE PENALIZER...IS **NO MORE!**

"I MESMERIZED HIM WITH THE **HYPNO-COIN** AND ERASED ALL MEMORY OF HIS EVIL **DOUBLE IDENTITY**..."
AAAAAAGH!

"...THOUGH PERHAPS I HAVE CONDEMNED HIM TO A FAR MORE **DISMAL FATE!**"

I AM AN ELEMENTARY SCHOOL PRINCIPAL, I AM AN ELEMENTARY SCHOOL PRINCIPAL...

FROM NOW ON, THE HYPNO-COIN STAYS HERE IN THE BARTCAVE WHERE IT CAN DO NO HARM!
BUT THINK OF ALL THE GOOD YOU COULD DO WITH IT! YOU COULD MAKE THE COMIC BOOK SHOP LOWER ITS PRICES ON BACK ISSUES! YOU COULD --

NO, MY FRIEND! EVER SINCE THE KRUSTY SMITH NOVELTY COMPANY ACCIDENTALLY SENT ME THIS OLD HYPNO-COIN -- THE LONG-BANNED ORIGINAL MODEL THAT ACTUALLY WORKS -- I'VE FEARED THAT IT COULD FALL INTO THE WRONG HANDS! I CAN NEVER TAKE THAT RISK AGAIN!
SUCH POWER IS TOO EASILY ABUSED...EVEN BY MYSELF!

HOWEVER, I WAS UNABLE TO RESIST GIVING SKINNER A CERTAIN POST-HYPNOTIC SUGGESTION AS A FINAL JEST...!

THE NEXT DAY...
ELEMENTARY
SPRINGFIELD
WELL, BART, YOU'RE OFF THE HOOK -- OUR FLAG HAS BEEN REPAIRED!

I'M GLAD OUR LITTLE TALK YESTERDAY SEEMS TO HAVE DONE SOME GOOD!
NOW IF YOU'LL EXCUSE ME, I HAVE A SUDDEN UNEXPLAINABLE URGE TO INSPECT THE TEACHERS' LOUNGE!
HEH HEH!

OH, FOR HEAVEN'S SAKE, PEOPLE! CAN'T YOU CLEAN UP AFTER YOURSELVES? IT LOOKS LIKE A BARNYARD IN HERE--!
TEACHERS' LOUNGE
BARNYARD?!
DID SOMEONE SAY BAR--BAW--BWAK!

CLUCK CLUCK
BWAAK! BUKKAW!
COCK-A-DOODLE-DOOOOO
WHAT TH--?
CONTROL YOURSELVES, PEOPLE! WHAT ARE YOU DOING? GET OFF THAT EGG IMMEDIATELY! PEOPLE--!
THE END!

BONGO COMICS GROUP
PART 1 OF "WHEN BONGOS COLLIDE" CROSSOVER!
WITH SPECIAL GUEST STAR BART SIMPSON!
#3
ITCHY & SCRATCHY
COMICS
#5
BONGO COMICS GROUP
SIMPSONS
COMICS
BONGO COMICS GROUP
BARTMAN
#3
MEETS RADIOACTIVE MAN

WHEN
BONGOS
COLLIDE!

ONCE UPON A TIME
NOT SO FAR AWAY...

SPLORCH!
THE END!

HEY, KIDS, WASN'T THAT GREAT?! DON'T GO AWAY -- WE'LL BE RIGHT BACK WITH ANOTHER ITCHY & SCRATCHY CARTOON RIGHT AFTER THIS SHAMELESS PLUG FOR NEW IMITATION-CHOCOLATEY-FLAVOR FROSTY KRUSTY FLAKES!

ALL RIIIGHT! ANOTHER HEAPING HELPING OF HARMLESS CARTOON VIOLENCE!
YOU KNOW, JUDGING BY HIS EXPRESSION AT THE END OF THAT LAST EPISODE, I'D ALMOST THINK SCRATCHY HAS ACHIEVED A ZEN-LIKE ACCEPTANCE OF HIS SITUATION!
...SO GIVE A HOOT -- BUY MY CEREAL!

VWOOOSH!
KACHANK!
HUH?! WHAT'S THAT NOISE ON THE ROOF?
AND NOW, BACK TO ITCHY & SC--ZZZKKK!

UH-OH! I GUESS THE SCOTCH TAPE HOMER USED TO PUT UP THE ANTENNA FINALLY GAVE OUT!
MAYBE WE CAN FIX IT! BUT WE'LL HAVE TO ACT FAST, OR WE'LL MISS THE SHOW!

C'MON, LISA! HOMER KEEPS HIS TOOLS IN THE BASEMENT!

ZZZZZZZZ

ZEEEZ

ZEEZE
AYE CARUMBA!
WHAT'S THAT WEIRD GLOW?!

ZZZZZZZZZ
MAGGIE!

ZZAK!

I *SEE IT*...

SPROINK!
...BUT I DON'T *BELIEVE IT!*

WOW! ITCHY AND SCRATCHY -- WREAKING HAVOC IN *OUR HOUSE!*
THIS IS SO *COOL!* MAYBE I CAN GET THEIR *AUTOGR--*
NAB

YIIIIEEE!!!
HEH HEH! GO GET HIM, ITCHY!
BZZRRR!

OWWW!
HEY! THIS ISN'T HARMLESS CARTOON VIOLENCE -- THIS IS REAL!

VRZZZZZZZZ!

SMASH!

BZZZRRRRRR
EEEK!
YIKES!
OUCH!
YEOW!

WOW.
FOR SOME REASON, I HAVE A FORBODING SENSE OF IMPENDING CATASTROPHE.
YEAH -- AND I HAVE THE FEELING SOMETHING BAD IS GONNA HAPPEN, TOO!
MOM AND DAD WILL NEVER BELIEVE THIS...

BART! WHAT HAVE YOU DONE, BOY?!
OH, MY...
Living Room
AYE CARUMBA!

ONE HASTY EXPLANATION LATER...
...SO THEN ITCHY AND SCRATCHY CRASHED THROUGH THE WALL AND RAN OFF DOWN THE STREET!
BART, YOU CAN'T HONESTLY EXPECT US TO BELIEVE THAT! IT'S NEAR-IMPOSSIBLE!

YOUR MOTHER'S RIGHT, BOY! YOU'VE VIOLATED A SACRED TRUST BY DAMAGING YOUR FAMILY'S HOME -- FOR WHICH YOU MUST DIE!
LOOK ON THE BRIGHT SIDE, HOMER -- AT LEAST THE TV CAME THROUGH UNSCATHED!

OOOOH -- HE'S GOT A POINT THERE, MARGE!
HOMER!
BART, THIS IS SERIOUS! UNTIL WE CAN THINK OF A SUITABLE PUNISHMENT, YOU'RE GROUNDED!

"...THAT MEANS YOU DON'T GET TO GO SEE KRUSTY THE CLOWN PERFORM AT THE NUCLEAR POWER PLANT THIS AFTERNOON! GO TO YOUR ROOM!"
:SIGH: EVEN THE LATEST INSTANT-CLASSIC ADVENTURE OF RADIOACTIVE MAN CAN'T TAKE MY MIND OFF THE FACT THAT I'M MISSING THE CORPORATE-SPONSORED-ENTERTAINMENT EVENT OF THE YEAR!
KNOCK KNOCK
REDUNDANT RADIOACTIVE MAN

SORRY MOM GROUNDED YOU, BART!
I TRIED TO TELL HER WHAT REALLY HAPPENED, BUT SHE THINKS I'M JUST BEING MY USUAL NOBLE SELF BY STICKING UP FOR YOU!
:GROAN:

WELL, AT LEAST MR. FLANDERS IS SURE TO BE AT THE POWER PLANT WITH HIS VIDEO CAMERA! MAYBE YOU CAN WATCH THE TAPE LATER!
OH, MAN! HAVING TO GO TO FLANDERS' HOUSE TO WATCH KRUSTY -- HOW LOW CAN I SINK?
MAXIMUM CARNAGE
REDUNDANT RADIOACTIVE MAN

LATER...
:SIGH: I BET I'M THE ONLY PERSON IN TOWN WHO'S NOT GOING...
HEY--!

--IF EVERYBODY'S AT THE POWER PLANT, THAT MEANS JUST ONE THING! THIS BURG'S WIDE OPEN FOR...

...EL BARTO!
BRAND X SPRAY PAINT

SOON...
--DILLY-DOODLY! NOW WE'RE ROLLING!

SILLY ME! GUESS I HAVEN'T GOTTEN THE HANG OF THIS NEW CAMCORDER -- I FORGOT TO FLIP THE OL' "STANDBY" SWITCHEROO!

STAND OVER THERE WITH YOUR MOM, KIDS -- I WANT TO GET A SHOT OF YOU IN FRONT OF THE STAGE-A-ROONY!
4TH ANNUAL ENERGY SQUANDERERS AWARDS AND
YO, NUKES COMEDY JAM

"THAT'S A DANDY PICTURE! NOW I'LL JUST PAN OVER THE CROWD..."

"GEE WHILLIKERS! IT LOOKS LIKE EVERY-DING-DANG-DOODLY-BODY IN SPRINGFIELD IS HERE! AND WITH THIS ZOOM LENS, I CAN SEE CLEAR TO THE BACK OF THE CROWD..."
CRUSTY

"...AND GOSHAROOTIES, IF IT ISN'T THE SIMPSONS FAMILY-DOODLY!"

HIDILLYHO, NEIGHBOR!
STUPID FLANDERS! HOW COME HE GETS TO BE RIGHT UP FRONT?!
MAYBE HE DIDN'T WASTE HALF AN HOUR HAGGLING WITH THAT BOOTLEG T-SHIRT VENDOR!

MARGE, THIS ISN'T JUST A T-SHIRT! IT'S A POP CULTURE ARTIFACT! AFTER TODAY, WE'LL STORE IT AWAY -- AND MAYBE SOMEDAY THIS MINT-CONDITION COLLECTIBLE WILL HELP PAY FOR LITTLE LISA'S COLLEGE EDUCATION!
CRUSTY
SPIGFIELD
1994

HMMM...I THINK IT MIGHT HAVE BEEN WISER TO PUT THAT $20 IN THE COMPANY SAVINGS PLAN, BUT...
LOOK -- THE SHOW'S STARTING!

GOOD AFTERNOON, EVERYONE -- I'M TROY MCCLURE! YOU PROBABLY REMEMBER ME FROM SUCH FILMS AS "THREE MEN AND A NUKE," AND THE SMASH-HIT INSTRUCTIONAL VIDEO, "KISS YOUR BUTT GOODBYE: POST-MELTDOWN EMERGENCY PROCEDURES!"

BEFORE WE START OUR SHOW, LET'S HAVE A BIG HAND FOR OUR SPONSOR, MONTGOMERY BURNS!
CLAP
CLAP
CLAP

WRETCHED HOI POLLOI! SMITHERS, GET THE NAMES OF THOSE WHO FAILED TO APPLAUD AND SEE THAT THEIR ELECTRIC RATES ARE RAISED IMMEDIATELY!
SEND IN THE KLOWN
JOHN: 11:35
YESSIR!

AND NOW HERE'S THE GUY YOU'VE ALL BEEN WAITING FOR -- THAT CLOWN-ABOUT-TOWN -- KRUSTY!
YAY!
CLAP
CLAP CLAP
HOORAY
WOO HOO!
CLAP
CLAP

IT'S AN HONOR TO PRESENT YOU AND CHANNEL 6 WITH THIS AWARD FOR BEING SPRINGFIELD'S MOST WASTEFUL ENERGY USERS! THAT AIR-CONDITIONED PARKING GARAGE OF YOURS REALLY CLINCHED IT!
I'M HAPPY TO BE HERE, TROY -- ESPECIALLY SINCE THE JUDGE RULED THAT THIS SHOW WOULD COUNT TOWARDS MY COMMUNITY SERVICE TIME!

HEY, KIDS -- A FUNNY THING HAPPENED TO ME ON THE WAY TO THE NUCLEAR POWER PLANT TODAY --
SKREEEEEE
KRASH!
YAAAAAAH!
WHAT TH--?!

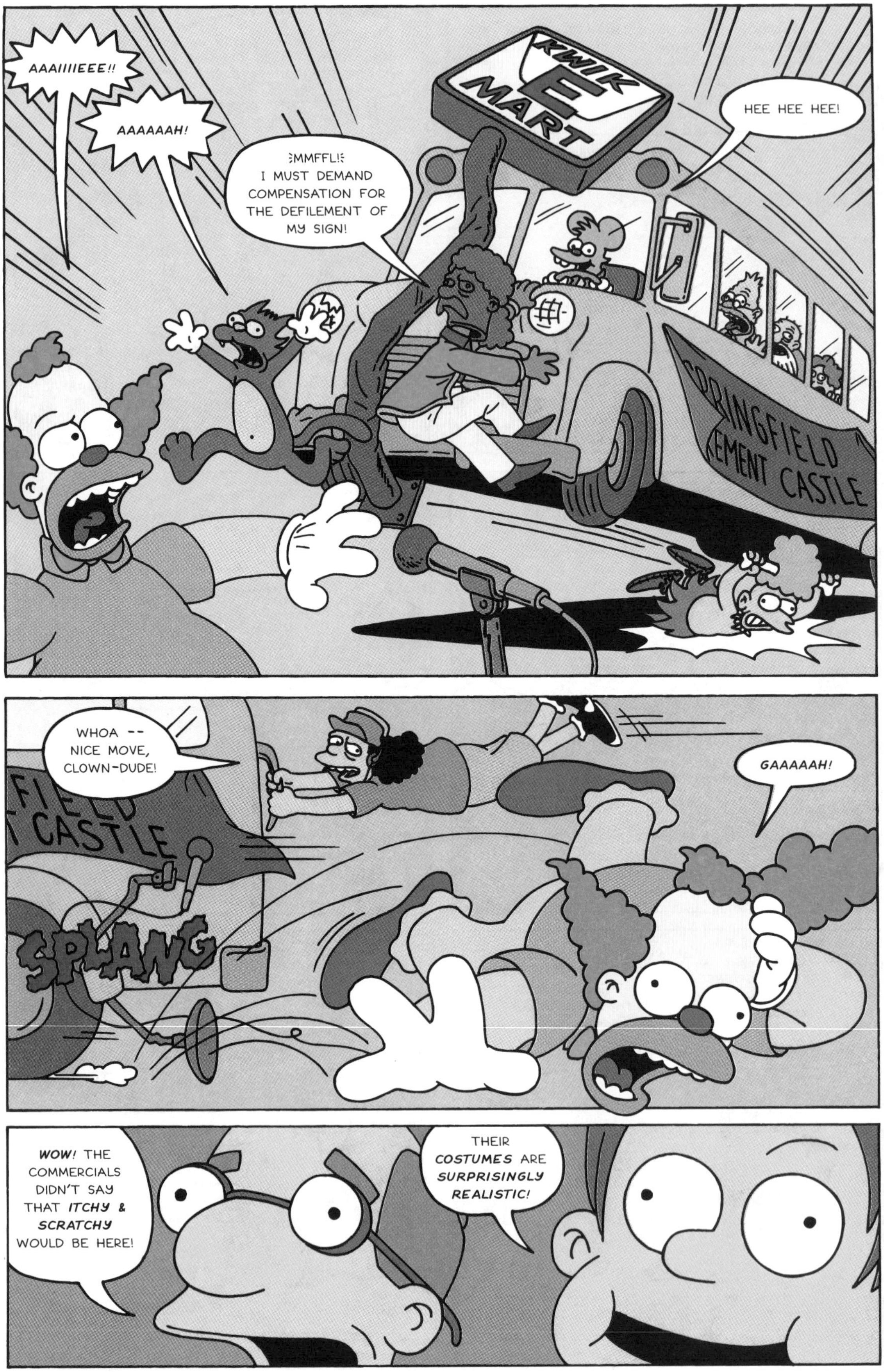

AAAIIIIEEE!!
AAAAAAH!
ƐMMFFL!Ʃ I MUST DEMAND COMPENSATION FOR THE DEFILEMENT OF MY SIGN!
HEE HEE HEE!
KWIK E MART

SPA-LAM!
SPLOINK
THIS CAT-AND-MOUSE FREAK SHOW WASN'T IN THE CONTRACT, YOU BLASTED MERRY-ANDREW -- YOU'LL NOT GET AN EXTRA PENNY FOR IT!

THEY'RE NOT PART OF MY ACT, YOU CRAZY OLD COOT! THEY'RE JUST SCENE-STEALERS!
HMMM...PRETTY GOOD COSTUMES, THOUGH!
OOOH...I NEED MY PILLS! I THOUGHT I SAW A GIANT BLUE RAT DRIVING THE BUS!

HA HA HA! OL' BURNS CAME THROUGH FOR ONCE -- THIS IS A GREAT SHOW!
YEAH -- NICE GOING, BURNS!

HOORAY FOR MR. BURNS!
YAAAAY!
BURNS! BURNS! BURNS!
LISTEN TO THEM, SMITHERS -- THAT THRONG OF REEDY VOICES LIFTED IN PRAISE OF THEIR BELOVED EMPLOYER...
AUTHORIZED PERSONNEL ONLY

...IN SPITE OF MY CONTEMPT FOR THEM, THEIR MINDLESS ADULATION WARMS MY HEART!
ANYTHING THAT WARMS YOUR HEART WARMS MY HEART TOO, SIR!
I HATE TO RAIN ON THIS PRECIOUS RAY OF SUNSHINE -- BUT I MUST!
IN CASE OF FIRE BREAK GLASS
REACTOR CORE

SIR, I'VE BEEN TRACKING THOSE TWO RATHER IRRESPONSIBLE CARTOON CHARACTERS SINCE THEY ENTERED THE PLANT, AND THEY MAY POSE A DANGER! SHALL I HAVE YOUR ESCAPE VEHICLE PREPARED?

EVACUATE -- IN MY MOMENT OF TRIUMPH?! I THINK YOU OVERESTIMATE THEIR DESTRUCTIVE CAPABILITIES!

WHAT IN THE NAME OF MALTHUS IS THAT?!
KA-SPLANG!
IT DOESN'T SOUND GOOD, SIR -- WE'D BETTER CHECK THE VIDEO MONITORS!

OH, DEAR! AS MUCH AS I WOULD LIKE TO SAVOR THIS MOMENT, I'M AFRAID WE'LL HAVE TO MOVE QUICKLY, SIR --

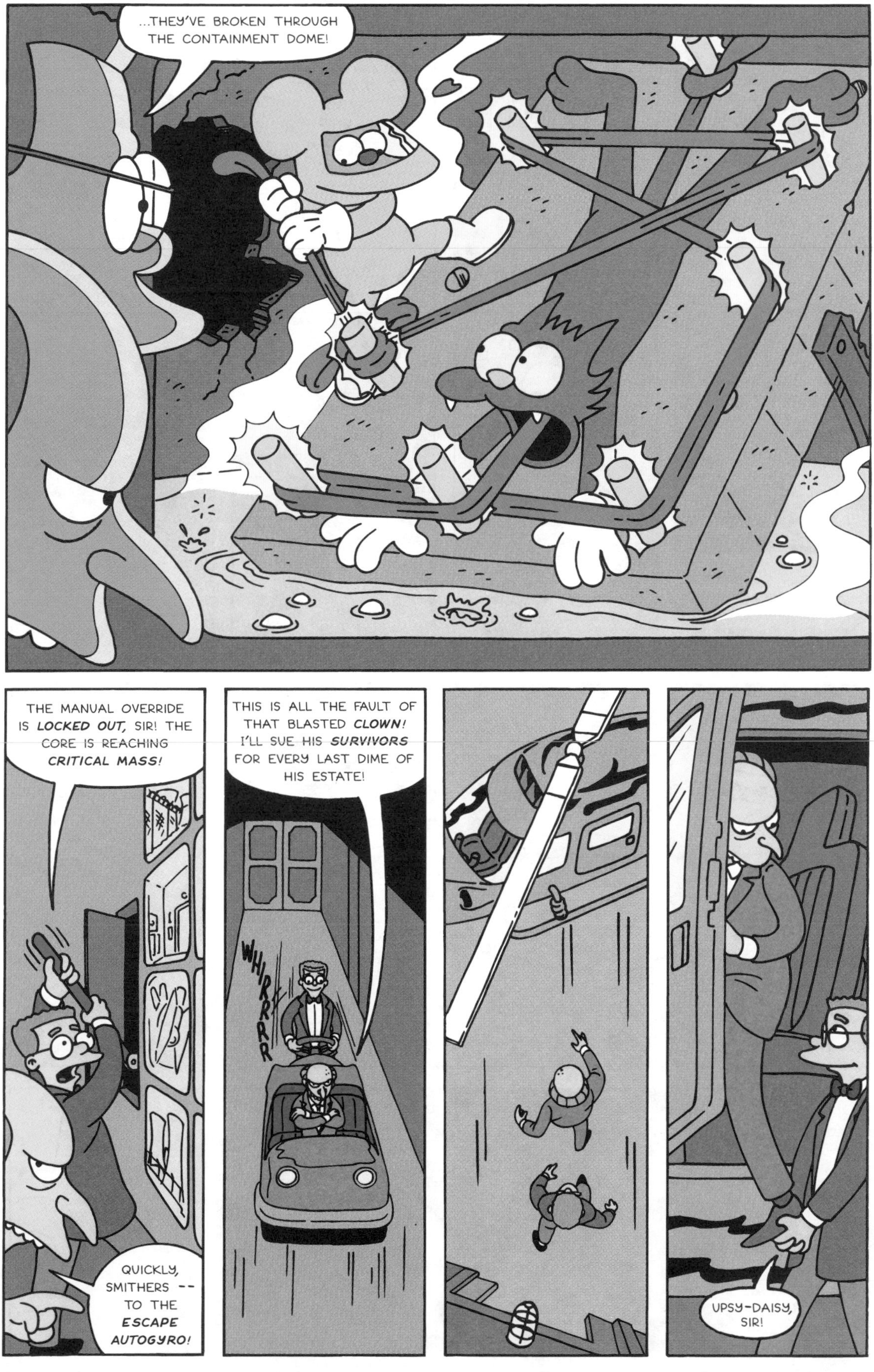

...THEY'VE BROKEN THROUGH THE CONTAINMENT DOME!

SLAM!
KLIK! LOCK!
WAIT, SIR! WHAT ABOUT ME?
OH, I AM SORRY, SMITHERS -- MY ENGINEERS SEEM TO HAVE NEGLECTED TO PROVIDE ACCOMODATIONS FOR YOU!

I'LL GLADLY CLING TO THE LANDING SKID, SIR!
HMMM...

VERY WELL -- BUT IF YOUR WEIGHT UNBALANCES THE CRAFT AND MAKES ME QUEASY, YOU'LL HAVE TO DROP OFF!
I WOULDN'T HAVE IT ANY OTHER WAY, SIR!

VUDDA VUDDA
I ONLY HOPE WE'RE IN TIME...

MEANWHILE...
EL BAR
ssss
MAN, THIS IS LIKE SHOOTING FISH IN A BARREL!
BUT SOMEHOW IT'S NOT QUITE THE SAME THRILL WITHOUT THE POSSIBILITY OF GETTING CAUGHT!

HEY, WHAT TH--?!

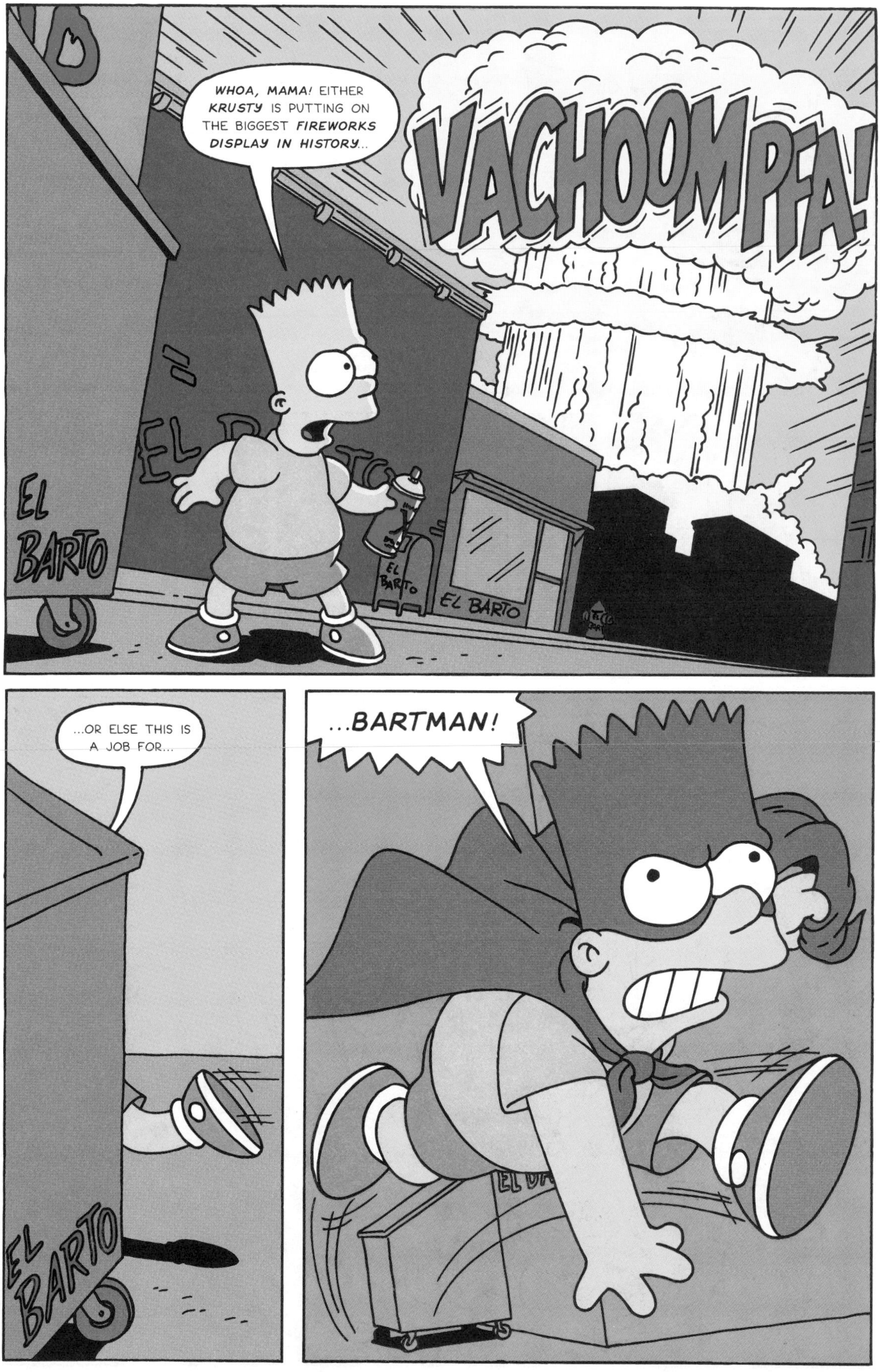

WHOA, MAMA! EITHER *KRUSTY* IS PUTTING ON THE BIGGEST *FIREWORKS DISPLAY IN HISTORY*...

VACHOOMPFA!

VACHOOMPFA!

GRACIOUS! I FEEL SO -- LIGHTHEADED...

WHAT'S HAPPENING TO ME?

I CAN FEEL MY BODY BURSTING WITH POWER --

I-I'M CHANGING!

CHANGING -- BUT INTO WHAT?!

THAT WEIRD GLOW...

FEEL SO -- STRANGE...

AHHH!

CAN THIS REALLY BE HAPPENING?

MEANWHILE...
MAN, THIS IS WEIRD! ZOOMING ACROSS AN EMPTY CITY TOWARDS A HUGE MUSHROOM CLOUD...
...THIS IS LIKE SOMETHING OUT OF AN ISSUE OF RADIOACTIVE MAN!

HMM...WHAT'S THAT UP AHEAD? IT ALMOST LOOKS LIKE...

NO...IT COULDN'T BE...

...AYE CARUMBA!! OF COURSE --!

-- A BUNCH OF NEW COSTUMED SUPER-CHARACTERS! IT'S THE INEVITABLE RESULT OF A NUCLEAR EXPLOSION!

ONE WAY
CRUSTY

GOT TO REMEMBER TO PROTECT MY SECRET IDENTITY!
WHAT'S GOING ON, MRS. SIMPSON? WHY ARE YOU DRESSED UP LIKE SOME SORT OF COSTUMED KOOK?

"MRS. SIMPSON"?
THERE IS NO MRS. SIMPSON! THERE IS ONLY --

--THE ENTANGLER!
YIKES! MY OWN MOM HAS BECOME AS SNARLY AND SHORT-TEMPERED AS A REAL COMIC-BOOK SUPER-CHARACTER!

YEOW!
THOOOF!
FWIK

UH-OH!

RRRAARR! ME AM -- THE INGESTIBLE BULK!
I SHOULD'VE KNOWN!

GRRRR! HOLD STILL, BITE-SIZED PURPLE ONE!

YOU MAKE BULK MAD, POINTY-HEAD!
AND THE ANGRIER BULK GETS --

-- THE HUNGRIER BULK GETS!
BULK GNASH!!

CHOMP!

MMMMM... CRUNCHY!
NOW -- WHILE HE'S GOT SOMETHING TO CHEW ON, I CAN GET OUTTA HERE!

WHOA!

THAT SOUND -- AND DAZZLING LIGHT! CAN BARELY SEE --
OH, NO! IT'S...

--LISA! AND THAT STUPID SAXAPHONE!!

OH, MAAAN...GET WITH IT! YOU'RE DIGGIN' THE JAZZLER!

MY AX IS, LIKE, MY VOICE, YOU DIG? IT'S HOW I EXPRESS MY TRUTH, MY PAIN, MY INNER HOWL...
YIKES -- SHE COULD GO ON LIKE THIS FOR HOURS! BUT AT LEAST WHILE SHE'S TALKING SHE CAN'T PLAY!

WHOOF!!

GRAMPA!?
BETTER WATCH OUT WHO YOU CALL "GRAMPA," YOU DURN WHIPPERSNAPPER! I'M FULLA VIM AND VINEGAR, I'VE GOT SUPERPOWERS TO SPARE--

-- AND I'M SPOILING FOR A FIGHT --
--ZZZZZZ--

COMA! WAKE UP, COMA!
ZZZZ
HUH?! WHUZZA?!
OH, YEAH...

THESE ARE MY TEAMMATES! BEDPAN --
THAT'S BADPAN, YOU OLD CODGER!
HE'S COMA -- I'M CODGER!
-- PHOGEY --
-- AND VAGUE!

TOGETHER, WE'RE CALLED --

HE'S FALLEN ASLEEP AGAIN!

I WASN'T SLEEPING -- I WAS PAUSING FOR DRAMATIC EFFECT!
NOW YOU'VE SPOILED IT!

AS I WAS SAYING, TOGETHER, WE'RE CALLED --
-- OLDBLOOD!

PRETTY STUPID NAME, MAN!
OOOOH...NOT ANOTHER PACK OF BRATS!
CLOSE, MAN -- WE'RE CALLED...WILDB.R.A.T.S!*
*WILD, BULLYING, ROWDY, ADOLESCENT TEAM -- S&C

COME ON, OLDBLOOD -- LET'S SHOW THESE PUERILE PUPS WHO'S THE TOP TEAM IN THESE PARTS!
HEY, SLACKER -- REMIND ME AGAIN WHY WE'RE FIGHTING THESE GUYS!
'CUZ WE'VE GOT SUPERPOWERS, MALL -- WHAT ELSE ARE WE GONNA DO BESIDES FIGHT?!
LET'S HAMMER THESE GEEZERS, SIMPLETON!
YOU GOT IT, SWITCHBLADE!
OH, MAN -- EVERYBODY IN TOWN EXCEPT ME GETS SUPERPOWERS -- AND I'M THE ONE WHO WINDS UP IN THE MIDDLE!

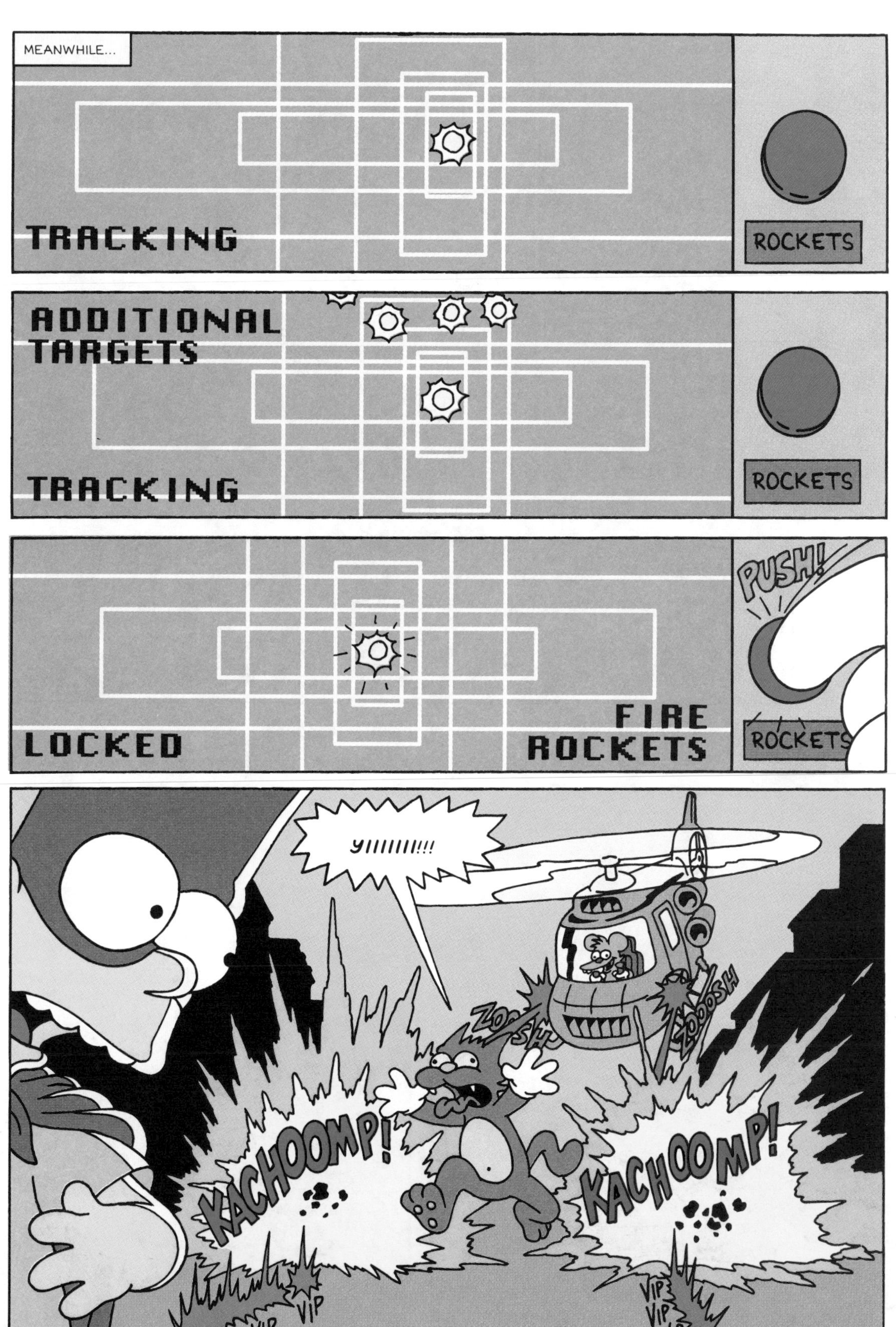
MEANWHILE...
TRACKING
ROCKETS
ADDITIONAL TARGETS
TRACKING
ROCKETS
LOCKED
FIRE ROCKETS
PUSH!
ROCKETS
YIIIIIII!!!
ZOOSH
ZOOOSH
KACHOOMP!
KACHOOMP!
VIP VIP VIP VIP
VIP VIP VIP VIP

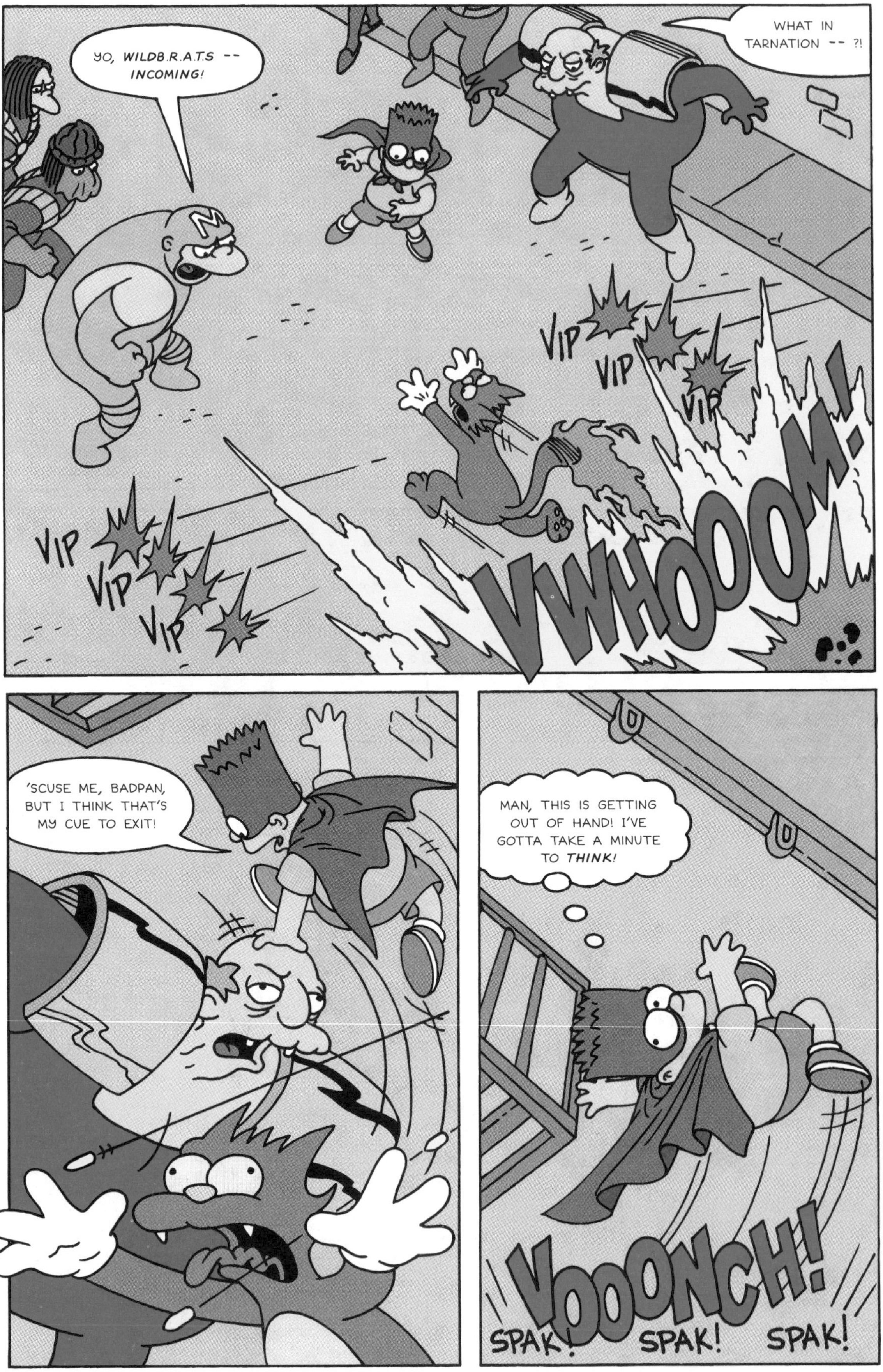

YO, WILDB.R.A.T.S -- *INCOMING!*
WHAT IN TARNATION -- ?!
VIP
VIP
VIP
VIP
VIP
VIP
VWHOOOOM!

'SCUSE ME, BADPAN, BUT I THINK THAT'S MY CUE TO EXIT!

MAN, THIS IS GETTING OUT OF HAND! I'VE GOTTA TAKE A MINUTE TO *THINK!*
VOOONCH!
SPAK!
SPAK!
SPAK!

HAS THE WORLD GONE CRAZY?! FIRST ITCHY & SCRATCHY JUMP OUT OF OUR TV, AND NOW SPRINGFIELD IS OVERRUN BY A BUNCH OF COSTUMED WEIRDOS ALL BEATING THE STUFFING OUT OF EACH OTHER!

I GUESS IT'S LIKE THEY SAY IN THE COMICS -- "WITH GREAT POWER COMES EVEN GREATER IRRESPONSIBILITY!"
JACK'S
SPANDEX CITY
"I AM THE KING!"

BRRRAAP!
WHAT AM I GONNA DO? I'M THE ONLY NORMAL PERSON LEFT -- THE ONLY ONE STANDING BETWEEN SPRINGFIELD AND UTTER CHAOS! IF I DON'T--
--HUH?!

SMEK!
PLOP!
MY BRAIN -- IT'S TINGLING! LIKE SOME SORT OF SIXTH SENSE!

SPA-DOINK!
I HAVE THE STRANGEST FEELING THAT I NEED TO GET HOME -- RIGHT AWAY!

SOMETHING TELLS ME THAT THE ANSWER TO ALL THIS IS CLOSER THAN I REALIZE!
COMING SOON!
ALIEN INVASION

SOON...
HOME! AT LEAST THINGS LOOK NORMAL HERE! BUT NOW WHAT DO I DO?

AYE CARUMBA!
A FLYING SAUCER...PARKED IN FLANDERS' BACK YARD!
THIS COULD EXPLAIN A LOT!

I ALWAYS SUSPECTED FLANDERS WAS AN ALIEN!

CAN'T SEE ANYTHING FROM HERE -- GUESS I'M JUST GONNA HAVE TO GET **CLOSER**...

LOOKS LIKE NOBODY'S HERE! MAYBE I CAN FIND A **CLUE** OR SOMETHING!

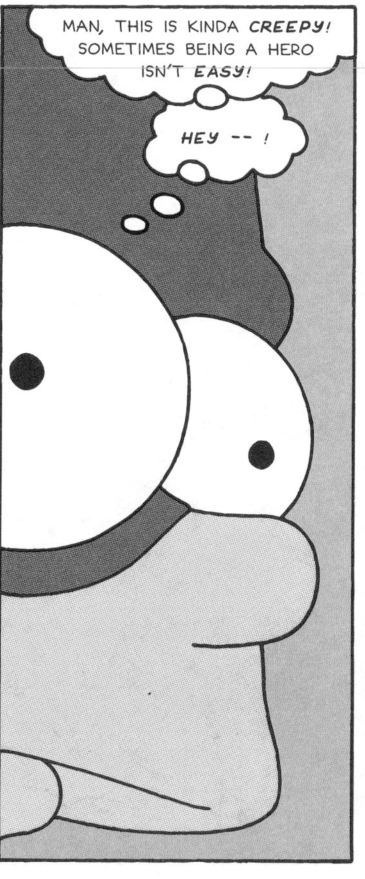
MAN, THIS IS KINDA **CREEPY**! SOMETIMES BEING A HERO ISN'T **EASY**!
HEY -- !

A **SCRATCHY MASK** -- LIKE THE GUY AT **KRUSTYLAND** WEARS! WHAT'S IT DOING **HERE**?!

BEHOLD, KODOS --
-- LUNCH!!
YIKES!

WAIT, KANG --!
UNNNHH!!

-- I PROMISED THE SPAWNLETS I'D BRING THEM A PET FROM THIS VOYAGE!
THIS SMALL, FEISTY ONE WHO SNEAKED ONTO OUR SHIP SEEMS FAR MORE ENTERTAINING THAN THE SPECIMEN WE COLLECTED EARLIER!

VERY WELL! HERE, EARTHLING, YOU MAY SHARE YOUR INCARCERATION WITH OUR OTHER CAPTIVE --
OOOF!

-- THE BLASPHEMOUS IMPOSTOR OF THE REVERED SCRATCHY!
WHAT TH--?! IT'S THE GUY FROM KRUSTYLAND!
"REVERED SCRATCHY"?! HEY--!
KLANG!
-- YOU MEAN YOU GUYS ARE ITCHY & SCRATCHY FANS?!

INSOLENT WHELP! YOU DARE QUESTION US?
HOLD, KANG -- FAILING TO ENGAGE IN EXPOSITORY CONVERSATION WOULD BE A BREACH OF EARTH ETIQUETTE IN A MOMENT SUCH AS THIS!

WELL, IN THAT CASE -- YES, WE OBSERVE ITCHY AND SCRATCHY'S ANTICS DAILY ON OUR VIDEO SCREENS! AFTER ALL, SENSELESS VIOLENCE IS THE CORNERSTONE OF RIGELIAN PHILOSOPHY!
ITCHY AND SCRATCHY HAVE BEEN A SOURCE OF GREAT EDIFICATION DURING OUR LENGTHY INTERSTELLAR VOYAGES! IT WAS THEY WHO INSPIRED OUR PILGRIMAGE TO EARTH!

YES -- WE WISHED TO BRING THEM BACK TO RIGEL-4 WITH US, SO THAT OUR BRETHREN MIGHT SHARE OUR ENLIGHTENMENT! WE SPENT MANY ROTATIONAL CYCLES SCANNING THE SURFACE OF YOUR PUNY WORLD IN SEARCH OF THEM -- BUT IN VAIN!

"AT LAST, WE THOUGHT WE HAD FOUND SCRATCHY -- BUT IT WAS MERELY THAT WRETCHED HUMAN IN DISGUISE!* IT WAS THEN THAT WE REALIZED THAT ADVANCED CONSCIOUSNESSES SUCH AS ITCHY AND SCRATCHY WOULD HAVE NO NEED FOR THE RESTRAINTS OF PHYSICAL FORM! THEY EXIST ON A METAPHYSICAL PLANE -- WHAT YOU CALL 'TELEVISION LAND!'"
KRUSTYLAND
*SEE SIMPSONS #4, PAGE 3, PANEL 5 -- S&C

THUS, WE SIMPLY HOVERED ABOVE THE NEIGHBORING DWELLING AND USED OUR TRANS-TEMPORAL REALITY-INTEGRATOR CANNON TO MATERIALIZE THEM FROM OUT OF THE HUMANS' TELEVISION!*
*SO THAT'S WHAT HAPPENED BACK IN I&S #3! -- S&C

THEN YOU'RE RESPONSIBLE FOR ITCHY AND SCRATCHY BLOWING UP THE NUCLEAR POWER PLANT AND TURNING ALL OF SPRINGFIELD'S CITIZENS -- EXCEPT ME -- INTO SUPER-POWERED HOOLIGANS!*
WE DO NOT DESERVE FULL CREDIT -- THAT ENTIRE AMUSING EPISODE WAS ACTUALLY AN UNANTICIPATED DIVIDEND! HA HA HA!
HA HA HA!
*SEE SIMPSONS #5 -- S&C

LOOK, KANG! OUR MONITORS HAVE LOCATED ITCHY AND SCRATCHY! SHALL WE GO OBSERVE THEIR HIJINKS?
FILE TAPE

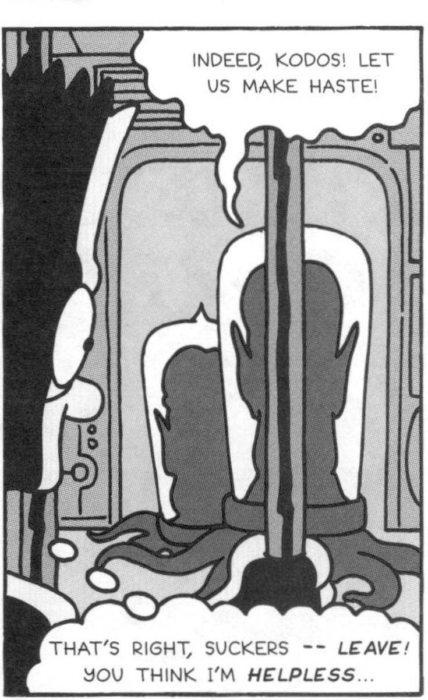
INDEED, KODOS! LET US MAKE HASTE!
THAT'S RIGHT, SUCKERS -- LEAVE! YOU THINK I'M HELPLESS...

...BUT I'VE GOT SOMETHING ELSE UP MY SLEEVE!

I'LL CONTACT MY PAL MILHOUSE WITH MY TWO-WAY SIGNAL WATCH! HE'LL RESCUE ME!
BARTMAN SIGNAL WATCH
ZEE
ZEE

MEANWHILE...
THUNK!

HA HA! GET READY FOR THE INDIAN BURN OF YOUR LIFE, WIMP!
IT'LL TAKE MORE THAN THAT TO DEFEAT --

-- THE SCARLET WHIMPERNEL!
HA! HE'S NO MATCH FOR MY SUPER WHINE!

I'VE LONG SUSPECTED THAT BULLY WAS JUST A COWARD AT HEART -- BUT I'VE ALWAYS BEEN TOO CHICKEN TO FIND OUT FOR SURE!
BUT WITH MY NEW POWERS -- EH?! BARTMAN'S SIGNAL! HE NEEDS ME!
ZEE
WELL, TOO BAD FOR HIM! THIS DREADED AVENGER IS GOING SOLO -- STARTING NOW!

AND SO...
GOSH -- I GUESS EVEN MY TRUSTED SIDEKICK MILHOUSE HAS BECOME AN IRRESPONSIBLE SUPER-JERK! WHAT AM I GOING TO DO?

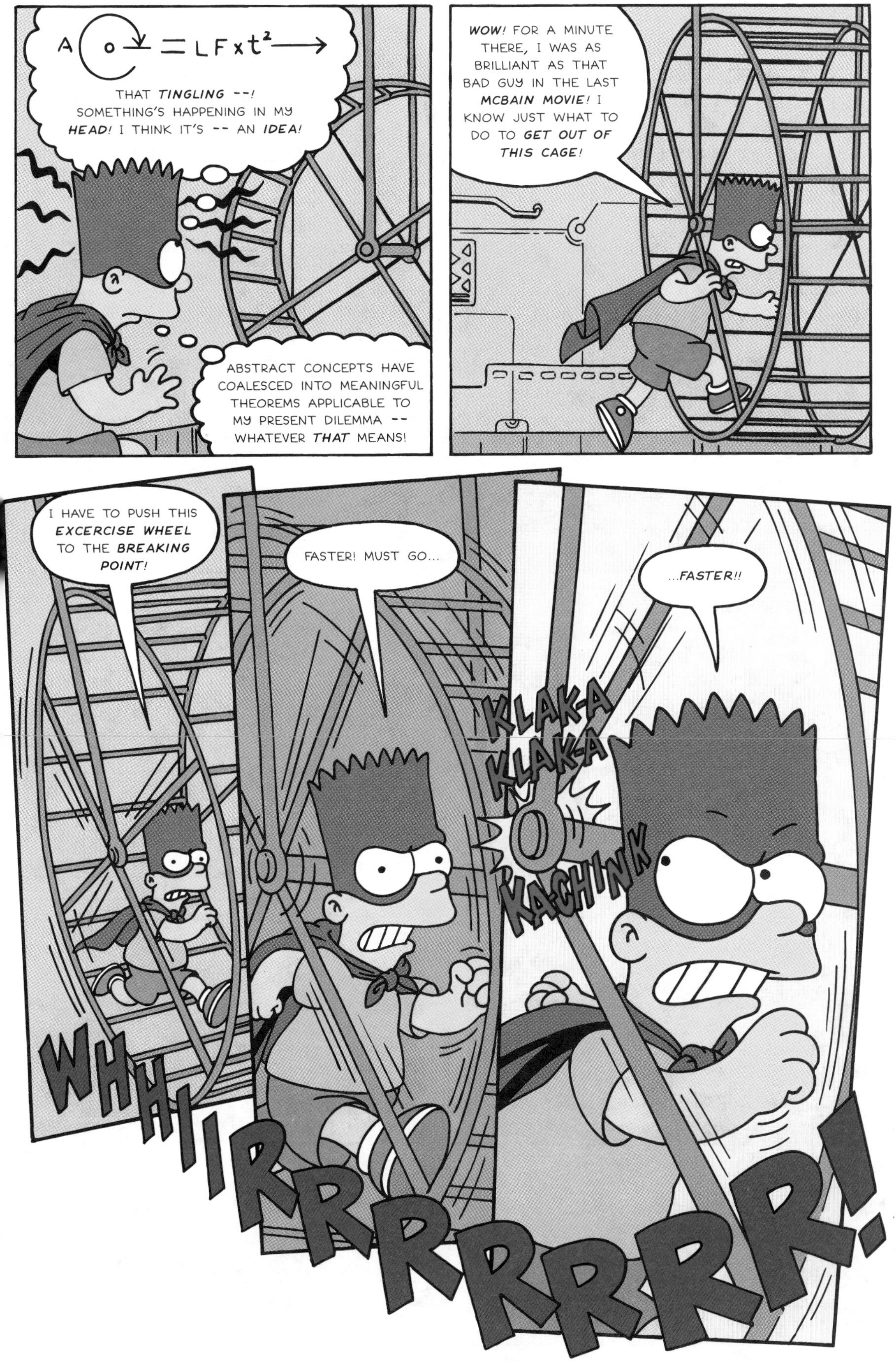

A o = LFxt² →
THAT *TINGLING* --! SOMETHING'S HAPPENING IN MY *HEAD!* I THINK IT'S -- AN *IDEA!*
ABSTRACT CONCEPTS HAVE COALESCED INTO MEANINGFUL THEOREMS APPLICABLE TO MY PRESENT DILEMMA -- WHATEVER *THAT* MEANS!

WOW! FOR A MINUTE THERE, I WAS AS BRILLIANT AS THAT BAD GUY IN THE LAST *MCBAIN MOVIE!* I KNOW JUST WHAT TO DO TO *GET OUT OF THIS CAGE!*

I HAVE TO PUSH THIS *EXCERCISE WHEEL* TO THE *BREAKING POINT!*
FASTER! MUST GO...
...*FASTER!!*
KLAK-A KLAK-A
KA-CHINK
WHHIIRRRRRR!

KLACHANG

WHEW! IF I'M GOING TO RESTORE ORDER TO SPRINGFIELD, MEND THE RIP IN THE TRANS-TEMPORAL REALITY CURTAIN, AND DEFEAT THE ALIEN MENACE, I'M GOING TO NEED SOME HELP...!

BE CONSIDERATE! WIPE YOUR DROOL OFF PLASMA SPANNER AFTER USE!

SOON...
JUST IN TIME FOR THE DAILY RERUN OF THE OLD ***RADIOACTIVE MAN*** TV SHOW!
KLIK
LARAMIE
MENTHOL

NOW, IF I UNDERSTOOD THAT BRAINWAVE OF MINE, ALL I HAVE TO DO NOW IS THROW THIS SWITCH...
OKAY, BEAK-BOY -- YOU ***ASKED FOR IT!***

ZZZAK!
POW

POW
SPROINK!

WHAT'RE YOU TRYING T' DO, DIRK -- BREAK MY JAW? YOU ACTUALLY ***CONNECTED*** WITH THAT PUNCH!
GEEZ, I'M SORRY, MEL! IT DIDN'T DO MY ***HAND*** ANY GOOD, EITHER!
POW
AHEM!

WELCOME TO THE ***REAL WORLD,*** GENTLEMEN!
???

…ER A LENGTHY EXPLANATION...
...SO YOU SEE, THE CITY IS IN *CHAOS!* IT'S UP TO *US* TO BRING SPRINGFIELD BACK TO NORMAL!
YOU'RE OUTTA YOUR *MIND,* KID! I'M A *TV STAR,* NOT A SUPERHERO!
YEAH! FORGET IT!

SORRY, JUNIOR, BUT IF I SOIL THE SUIT, THE DRY CLEANING COMES OUT OF MY *PAYCHECK!*
GOOD LUCK SAVING THE CITY!

C'MON, MEL! WE'RE IN THE MIDDLE OF A *CIVIL DISTURBANCE,* AND YOU KNOW WHAT *THAT* MEANS!
YEAH! SOMEWHERE, A BUNCH OF HOOLIGANS HAVE TAKEN OVER A *BAR!*
:SIGH:

FREE BEER FOR *EVERYBODY!* :*BELCH!*:
MOE'S

SO WHAT SUPER POWER DO *I* GET? STRENGTH? X-RAY VISION? *NO!* I GET TO BE *FOUR INCHES TALL!* THIS *STINKS!*
WHAT ARE YOU COMPLAINING ABOUT, *BARFLY?* WE LET YOU OUT OF THE *PINBALL MACHINE,* DIDN'T WE?

I SHOULD'VE KNOWN THAT PHONY-BALONEY *TV* RADIOACTIVE MAN WOULD WIMP OUT ON ME! THERE'S ONLY ONE *TRUE* RADIOACTIVE MAN...!

...THE ONE IN THE COMIC BOOK! IF ONLY HE WAS ON TV!
RADIOACTIVE MAN

UNTIL THIS MOMENT, I WAS GLAD RADIOACTIVE MAN HAD NEVER HAD ONE OF THOSE STUPID, ULTRA-CHEAPO CARTOON SHOWS THAT WAS SHOT STRAIGHT FROM THE COMIC BOOKS! BUT NOW --
I HOPE YOU STILL HAVE YOUR SUPERIOR SQUAD MEMBERSHIP CARD!
OF COURSE! I HAVE IT RIGHT HERE!
WELCOME BACK, RM!
THE END!

HEY! I'VE JUST HAD ANOTHER BRILLIANT IDEA!

SOON...
WITH HOMER'S OLD VIDEO CAMERA, I CAN FEED AN IMAGE OF THE COMIC BOOK RADIOACTIVE MAN INTO THE TV! THEN I CAN USE THAT ALIEN GIZMO TO MATERIALIZE HIM...
...I HOPE!
BETA

I WONDER IF THERE'S SOME SECRET ENTITY BEHIND THESE MYSTERIOUS INSPIRATIONS OF MINE! OR MAYBE, DUE TO RESIDUAL RADIATION, I'VE GAINED SOME STRANGE NEW MENTAL POWER...
KLIK

STOP! DON'T PULL THAT SWITCH!
FALLOUT BOY IS INNOCENT -- AND I CAN PROVE IT!

WAIT A MINUTE! THIS ISN'T DEATH ROW AT ZENITH MAXIMUM SECURITY PRISON!
WHAT TH--?!
WELCOME TO THE REAL WORLD, RADIOACTIVE MAN!

AFTER ANOTHER LENGTHY EXPLANATION...
LOOK, RM! IT'S CHAOS OUT THERE!
:GASP: I HAVEN'T SEEN SUCH A SENSES-SHATTERING SLUGFEST SINCE THE SECRET CRISIS ON ERSATZ EARTHS!
SOK
KRAK

THIS BLATANT DISREGARD FOR PRIVATE PROPERTY MUST BE STOPPED!
I'LL RESTORE ORDER TO SPRINGFIELD, OR MY NAME ISN'T CLAUDE KANE III!
KRASH!
BIFF

...ER, WHICH IT ISN'T, OF COURSE!
WHEW! ALMOST REVEALED MY SECRET IDENTITY!
HMMM...I WONDER IF I SHOULD TELL RM THAT, THANKS TO READING HIS COMICS, I KNOW ALL HIS SECRETS!

SOON, AT THE NUCLEAR POWER PLANT...
BY THE BUNS OF BURNS! I, **THE MIGHTY SMITER**, AM SURROUNDED BY THE RENEGADE **FISSION DIVISION**!
E'EN **MY** GREAT POWER IS NOT ENOUGH TO DEFEAT THESE MISCREANTS!

THERE IS NAUGHT BUT ONE THING TO DO, THOUGH IT DEFIES EVERY PRINCIPLE OF PHYSICS! I MUST TWIRL FAITHFUL **KJOHLER**, MY KEY TO THE **EXECUTIVE WASHROOM**...

...THEN **CAST IT SKYWARD**, NEGLECTING TO **LET GO**, THEREBY ACHIEVING **FLIGHT**!
HOLD IT, GOLDILOCKS...!

...THIS IS FOR **BREAKING THE LAWS OF PHYSICS**!
SMEK

RM! THE **FISSION DIVISION**...THEY'RE GETTING AWAY!
EH?!

THIS SECTION OF RAILROAD TRACK WILL DO THE TRICK!
SPROINK!

YAAAAH!
NOW TO CORRAL THOSE LONG-ARMED MALCONTENTS!
KERASH!

YOU FISSION BOYS WEREN'T TRYING TO SPLIT ON ME, WERE YOU?
HA! THE RAZOR WIT IS AS SHARP AS EVER!
GLURK
EEP
WHOOF
SKREEK!

MEANWHILE...
AYE CARUMBA!

GO AHEAD AN' SQUEAL, YE BLASTED PIGBOY! 'TWILL NOT SAVE YE FROM...THE PLAID PIPER!
MAN, HOW IRONIC! THIS IS JUST THE KIND OF MINDLESS FIGHT SCENE I'D ENJOY IF IT WERE IN A COMIC BOOK -- BUT NOW I HAVE TO TRY AND STOP IT!
FACE THE DANG-DIDDLY-DREADFUL WRATH OF...CAPTAIN KEEN, YOU MEANIE!
YOU CAN'T ESCAPE...THE HUMAN TORQUE, DUDE!
YOU'LL NEVER DEFEAT...THE STICKLER!
CAPTAIN KWIK MUST RESPECTFULLY DISAGREE, MALEFACTOR!

SOMEHOW I MUST --
WHAT TH --?!
FWIP!
FWIP!

OUR MAGIC JUMP ROPES FORCE YOU TO OBEY THE COMMANDS OF THE MIRROR MAIDENS, BARTMAN!
FROM NOW ON, YOU WILL WEAR YOUR UNDERWEAR ON THE OUTSIDE OF YOUR PANTS! TEE HEE!
LOSING MY WILL... TO RESIST!

NORMALLY IT'S CONTRARY TO MY CODE TO USE MY SUPER-STRENGTH AGAINST YOUNG GIRLS --
-- BUT THIS TIME IT'S EXPEDIENT!
BASH
WHAM
RADIOACTIVE MAN!

THANKS FOR RESCUING ME, RM! I'VE HAD ENOUGH OF ALL THESE CHARACTERS -- LET'S CLEAN UP THIS BURG!
RIGHT!

AND SO BEGINS A SYNAPSE-SCORCHING, INSURANCE-COMPANY-BANKRUPTING BATTLE SUCH AS SPRINGFIELD HAS NEVER SEEN BEFORE!
HAHAHA! THE JOKESTER ALWAYS HAS THE LAST LAUGH, RADIOACTIVE CHUMP!
WHOOPS!
NO ONE ESCAPES UNSOILED FROM...THE MUDSLINGER!
SPLUT
AYE CARUMBA! MY FOE HAS SPLIT INTO THREE SEPARATE PEOPLE!
I, THE SEQUELIZER, CAN CREATE AN INFINITE NUMBER OF COPIES OF MYSELF -- ALTHOUGH EACH IS ONLY 50% AS POWERFUL AS THE ONE BEFORE...
YAAAAH! GET AWAY!
DO NOT STRUGGLE, MORTAL! YOU CANNOT RESIST...VAMPIREDNA!
NOOOO!

QUITE A WHILE LATER...
THERE'S *TOO MANY* SUPER-POWERED SPRINGFIELDIANS TO STOP THEM ALL WITH *BRUTE FORCE*!
YEAH! AND THAT *MUD GUY* -- *YECCH*!
I GUESS IF WE CAN'T FIGHT 'EM HARDER, WE'LL JUST HAVE TO FIGHT 'EM *SMARTER*!

THUD!
POW!
URF!
KRUNCH! KRUNCH! KRUNCH!
BLOOEY!
KRASH!
WHOMP!
AAAIIEE!

ZZORCH!
PING! PING! PING!
VOOMP!
CHUD!
SPLORCH
BLAT!
THOOM! THOOM
THOOM!

THOOEY!
GLOP GLOP
A-BOMB
VAK! VAK! VAK!
THOK!
BASH! VOPP!

I THINK I CAN TAKE THAT GUY IN THE BABY-BLUE TIGHTS....
THERE'S MORE RAILROAD TRACKS OVER THERE...
KAPWEENG!
HOOMPH! SKUDGE!
BLORT!

OH, LET'S FACE IT...WE'RE AS HELPLESS TO STOP THIS CRISIS AS YOU WERE TO PREVENT WORLD WAR III IN ISSUE #157!
OF COURSE, THAT WAS JUST AN IMAGINARY STORY -- THIS IS REAL LIFE!
NUCLEAR CONDITIONS
ALL IS WELL!
HEY, LOOK...
...IT'S FLANDERS' VIDEO CAMERA! MAYBE I'LL GET TO SEE KRUSTY'S LIVE SHOW AFTER ALL!*
PROP. NED FLANDERS
*FLANDERS WAS TAPING THE ACTION IN SIMPSONS #5 -- S&C
AND TO THINK, JUST A FEW SHORT HOURS AGO, THIS WAS SPRINGFIELD!
ORDINARY PEOPLE IN A TOWN LIKE ANY OTHER, THEIR PENT-UP HOSTILITY HELD IN CHECK BY IMPOTENCE AND FEAR!
KRUSTY
PLAY
HOLD ON!
I'M GETTING ANOTHER BRILLIANT INSPIRATION!
???

SOON...
I'M BACK, BARTMAN!
GOOD! ARE YOU SURE THAT'S THE *HYPER-SPATIAL FLUX DRIVE* FROM THE ALIENS' SHIP?

IT'S THE HYPER-THING, ALL RIGHT! SOME GUY IN A *CAT SUIT* POINTED IT OUT TO ME!
OKAY! PLUG IT IN TO THE TRANS-TEMPORAL REALITY INTEGRATOR AND LET'S GET THIS SHOW ON THE ROAD!

MOMENTS LATER...
THERE! THAT'S THE LAST OF THE CONNECTIONS!
ACCORDING TO MY LATEST BRAINSTORM, BY USING FLANDERS' TAPE AS A SAMPLING REFERENCE, WITH A SIMPLE ADJUSTMENT OF THE TIME-BASE CORRECTOR I CAN RETURN US ALL TO THE MOMENT BEFORE ITCHY AND SCRATCHY MATERIALIZED, THUS UNDOING ALL THE ENSUING MAYHEM!

HOW DO YOU KNOW IT WON'T *BLOW UP,* IGNITE EARTH'S ATMOSPHERE, AND DESTROY ALL LIFE ON THE PLANET?
HEY, IF THE INVENTORS OF THE *ATOM BOMB* DIDN'T WORRY ABOUT IT, WHY SHOULD I?

BUT BEFORE BARTMAN CAN PULL THE LEVER...
OH, MAN -- NOT *ANOTHER* HOLE IN THE WALL!
VRROOOZZZ

AH-HA! SO *THIS* IS WHERE OUR *MOLECULAR DESTABILIZER* WENT!
THANK GROD YOU DIDN'T PULL THAT LEVER! IT WOULD HAVE *BLOWN UP,* IGNITED THE ATMOSPHERE, AND DESTROYED ALL LIFE ON THE PLANET!

MOLECULAR DESTABILIZER?! WE THOUGHT IT WAS THE HYPER-SPATIAL FLUX DRIVE!

SILLY HUMAN! THIS IS THE HYPER-SPATIAL FLUX DRIVE! WE ALWAYS TAKE IT WITH US WHEN WE LEAVE THE SHIP TO PREVENT THE THEFT OF OUR CRAFT!

OUR SECURITY MEASURES ARE QUITE EXTENSIVE!

BUT ENOUGH BANTER! THIS IS THE PENALTY FOR THIEVERY ON RIGEL-4!
OOOOF!
VROOZZ
RADIOACTIVE MAN! NOOO!

TOO BAD! YOU WOULD HAVE MADE A MOST EDUCATIONAL TEST SUBJECT FOR THE SPAWNLETS' SCIENCE PROJECT!
GULP
UH -- KLAATU BARADA NIKTO, MAN?

THAT WHINE -- LIKE TENTACLE-TIPS SLIDING DOWN A BISPECTRAL CARBONATE DISPLAY MATRIX!
MY SPACE HELMET IS VIBRATING!
EEEEEEEEEEEEE

NO! OUR RIGELIAN COMPLEXIONS CAN'T TOLERATE THE EARTH ATMOSPHERE!
IT DISSOLVES US INTO REPULSIVE PUDDLES OF SMELLY GOO!
EEEEEEEEEEEEEEEEE
KRACHANG!
SKLASH!
YAAAAAAAA!
AAAIIIEEE!
WOW!
THIS TIME-REVERSAL THING HAD BETTER WORK -- OR MOM'S GONNA KILL ME WHEN SHE SEES THIS MESS!
BUT WHERE DID THAT HELMET-SHATTERING WHINE COME FROM?
FROM ME, BARTMAN...

...THE SCARLET WHIMPERNEL!
MILHOUSE!

YOU DIDN'T ABANDON ME AFTER ALL!
NO, BARTMAN! I LEARNED THAT BEING A LONE VIGILANTE IS...LONELY!

I'D LIKE TO RETURN TO MY RIGHTFUL PLACE AT YOUR SIDE...IF YOU'LL HAVE ME, THAT IS!
I WOULDN'T WANT IT ANY OTHER WAY, OLD FRIEND!

WE'VE DEFEATED THE ALIENS -- BUT AT SUCH A TERRIBLE COST! RADIOACTIVE MAN IS --
OOOOH!

-- HE'S ALIVE! I SHOULD HAVE KNOWN! HE ALWAYS COMES BACK IN THE COMICS!
BOY, THOSE ALIEN DEATH RAYS ALWAYS GIVE ME SUCH A HEADACHE...

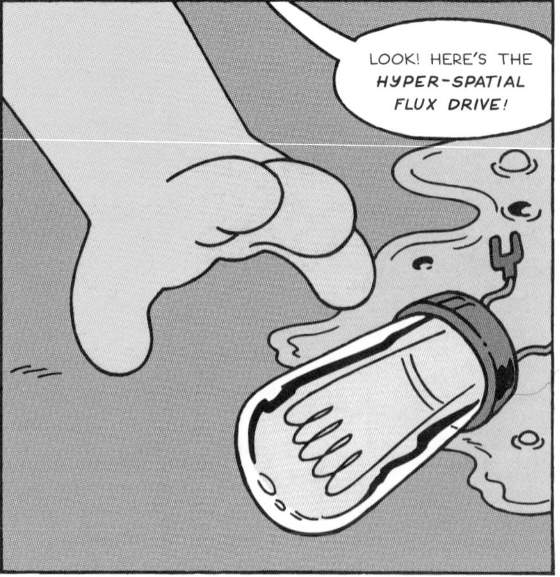
LOOK! HERE'S THE HYPER-SPATIAL FLUX DRIVE!

HERE, RM -- YOU KNOW WHAT TO DO NOW!
I SURE DO!

CONNECT IT TO THE TRANS-TEMPORAL REALITY-INTEGRATOR CANNON!
RIGHT!

MOMENTS LATER...
OKAY, EVERYTHING'S SET! HERE GOES!
WAIT, BARTMAN! BEFORE YOU RESTORE SPRINGFIELD AND WE ALL CONVENIENTLY FORGET EVERYTHING THAT HAPPENED, I WANT TO GIVE YOU SOMETHING!

I WAS GOING TO ENSHRINE THIS IN THE TROPHY ROOM OF MY CONTAINMENT DOME, BUT NOW I'D LIKE YOU TO HAVE IT!
RADIOACTIVE MAN'S SUPERIOR SQUAD MEMBERSHIP CARD!

I WON'T BE NEEDING IT ANYMORE...SINCE MY MEMBERSHIP WAS :CHOKE: REVOKED!
AYE CARUMBA! LITTLE DOES RM KNOW THAT HIS DISMISSAL FROM THE SUPERIOR SQUAD WAS JUST A CLEVER PLOY TO FOOL FALLOUT BOY'S TWIN BROTHER DODD, WHOSE MIND WAS WARPED BY BRUTAL HAZING AT MILITARY SCHOOL!
RM IS REINSTATED WITH HONORS JUST A FEW PAGES AFTER THE PANEL I MATERIALIZED HIM FROM!

VWOOSH!

TARGET IN RANGE...

BOMB RELEASE
...**BUMS AWAY!** HEE HEE HEE!

THANK YOU, **RM,** AND REMEMBER... THINGS ARE ALWAYS DARKEST BEFORE THE SURPRISE REVELATION ON PAGE 20!
THANK YOU, BARTMAN!
NOW I'D BETTER HURRY UP AND SEND EVERYONE BACK WHERE THEY BELONG!

JUST ONE THING STILL PUZZLES ME!
I'M **NEVER** GONNA GET TO PULL THIS DARNED LEVER!
WHAT'S THAT, **RM**?

WHAT WAS THE MYSTERIOUS SOURCE BEHIND YOUR BRILLIANT INSPIRATIONS?

YEEEEOW!!
A-BOMB

A-BOMB

AAAAAAAA

OH, ***THAT!*** I FIGURED IT OUT AWHILE BACK! I JUST HAD TO KEEP IT A SECRET FOR THE SAKE OF ***DRAMATIC TENSION!***
ALLOW ME TO INTRODUCE...

...***BRAINBABY*** -- FORMERLY MY KID SISTER, MAGGIE!
SHE GAINED AWESOME MENTAL POWERS FROM THE EXPLOSION, BUT SHE STILL CAN'T ***TALK,*** SO SHE COMMUNICATED WITH ME ***TELEPATHICALLY!***
JEEPERS! SHE MUST BE NEARLY AS POWERFUL AS MY OLD ENEMY, ***BRAIN-O!***

NOW TO PULL THIS LEVER BEFORE ***SOMETHING ELSE*** HAPPENS!

ZZAK

LISA! MAGGIE! THEY'RE NORMAL AGAIN -- OR AS NORMAL AS THEY'RE EVER GONNA GET!
YOU KNOW, JUDGING BY HIS EXPRESSION AT THE END OF THAT LAST EPISODE, I'D ALMOST THINK SCRATCHY HAS ACHIEVED A ZEN-LIKE ACCEPTANCE OF HIS SITUATION!
...SO GIVE A HOOT -- BUY MY CEREAL!

AND ITCHY & SCRATCHY ARE BACK ON TV WHERE THEY BELONG!
WHOA! IT WORKED!

VWOOSH!
KACHANK!
WATCH WHERE YOU'RE GOING, KANG! YOU STRUCK THE ANTENNA ON THE ROOF OF THE DWELLING!

UH-OH! THAT NOISE! IT MUST BE THE ALIENS -- I GUESS THEY'RE BACK TOO! AND THEY'RE GOING TO MATERIALIZE ITCHY AND SCRATCHY AGAIN!
AND NOW, BACK TO ITCHY & SC--ZZZKKK!

HOLD THE CRAFT STEADY, KANG, SO I MAY FOCUS THE TRANS-TEMPORAL REALITY INTEGRATOR CANNON ON THE HUMANS' TELEVISION!

OH, NO! LOOK AT THE TV!
MAYBE WE CAN FIX IT! BUT WE'LL HAVE TO ACT FAST, OR WE'LL MISS THE SHOW!
AYE CARUMBA! IT'S STARTING ALL OVER! I'VE GOTTA STOP IT -- BUT HOW?!

ALL IS IN READINESS! LET US PREPARE TO WELCOME ITCHY AND SCRATCHY INTO OUR CONTINUUM!
ZZAK

BART! WHY ARE YOU TURNING IT OFF?!
WHO CARES ABOUT WATCHING STATIC? BESIDES, I'VE SEEN THIS ONE BEFORE!
KLIK

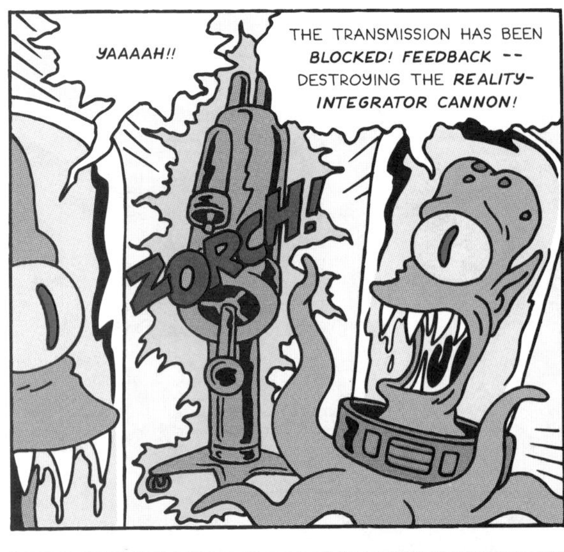
YAAAAH!!
THE TRANSMISSION HAS BEEN BLOCKED! FEEDBACK -- DESTROYING THE REALITY-INTEGRATOR CANNON!
ZORCH!

PHAGH! WE HAVE WASTED TOO MUCH TIME ON THIS BACKWATER PLANET IN PURSUIT OF ITCHY & SCRATCHY!
I CONCUR! I AM BEAMING DOWN THE BLASPHEMOUS SCRATCHY IMPOSTOR! LET US PROCEED TO ARCTURUS-7 TO OBSERVE THE ANTICS OF GLUEY, SHREWY, & KABLOOEY!

WHAT IN THE WORLD --? I'VE NEVER SEEN BART SO UNCONCERNED ABOUT MISSING ITCHY & SCRATCHY!
WHERE ARE YOU GOING?
I'VE GOTTA GO READ A COMIC BOOK!

WELCOME BACK TO ACTIVE DUTY, RADIOACTIVE MAN!
I HOPE YOU STILL HAVE YOUR SUPERIOR SQUAD MEMBERSHIP CARD!
IT'S GONE! BUT I DIDN'T... I DON'T REMEMBER... I'D NEVER...!
HA HA! DON'T WORRY, RM! THE SQUAD WILL BE HAPPY TO GIVE YOU A NEW ONE!
IT'S TRUE! IT ALL REALLY DID HAPPEN!
AND I'M THE ONLY ONE WHO KNOWS!

ELSEWHERE...
PERSONNEL OFFICE
KRUSTYLAND
YOU GOT A LOTTA NERVE, KID! FIRST YOU DISAPPEAR FOR TWO WEEKS, THEN YOU SHOW UP AND EXPECT US TO BELIEVE THIS CRAZY STORY ABOUT BEING KIDNAPPED BY ALIENS! YOU'RE FIRED!
JEEPERS!
THE END!

1. The Plaid Piper
2. Radioactive Man
3. Brainbaby
4. The Black Belch
5. The Jokester
6. Coma
7. Barfly
8. The Mudslinger
9. The Jazzler
10. Simpleton

11. The Penalizer
12. Bartman
13. Vampiredna
14. The Ingestible Bulk
15. Piggum
16. The Entangler
17,19. The Mirror Maidens
18. The Scarlet Whimpernel